Mario Vargas Llosa: Critical Essays on Characterization

𝔖cripta 𝔥umanistica

Directed by
BRUNO M. DAMIANI
The Catholic University of America

ADVISORY BOARD

Mario Vargas Llosa:
Critical Essays on Characterization

R. A. Kerr

𝔖cripta 𝔥umanistica

72

Library of Congress Cataloging in Publication Data

Kerr, R. A. (Roy A.)
    Mario Vargas Llosa : critical essays on characterization / by R. A. Kerr
        p.   cm. --(Scripta Humanistica (Series) ; 72)
        ISBN 0-916379-78-7 : $43.50
        1. Vargas Llosa, Mario, 1936-   --Characters.   I. Series
    PQ8498.32.A65Z69 1990
    863--dc20   90-4199
                                             CIP

Published by
Scripta Humanistica
1383 Kersey Lane
Potomac, Maryland 20854

For my parents

Paul L. Kerr (1917-1980) and Regina D. Kerr

and

(of course)

for

Annie

Acknowledgements

I would like to express my gratitude to all those who have made it possible for me to complete this project. I am most grateful to my mentors, Professors Terry J. Peavler, Leon F. Lyday, and Martin F. Stabb, all of The Pennsylvania State University. I extend thanks and appreciation to Professor Edward E. Borsoi, Rollins College, for his encouragement and advice, and to Ms Jane Wood, Rollins College, for assistance in the preparation of the manuscript. Publication of this study was made possible through a Rollins College Jack. B.Critchfield Summer Research Grant

Portions or versions of some of the essays in this collection have appeared previously in the following journals: Chasqui, Romance Notes, Hispanófila, Prismal/Cabral, Revista de estudios hispánicos, South Atlantic Review, Ideas '92.

Table of Contents

Introduction

Character at the Crossroads

Character is the driving force of fiction. --Leon Surmelian, <u>Techniques of Fiction</u> <u>Writing</u>

L'analyse structurale a eu la plus grand repugnance a traiter le personnage comme une essence..."--Roland Barthes, "Introduction à l'analyse structurale des récits"

In Book Six of the <u>Poetics</u>, Aristotle states that "it is the action which is the object of imitation; the individual characters are subsidiary to it."[1]   Until recently, this prescriptive analysis of the role of character in Drama and Epic has not been applicable to prose fiction. <u>Homo fictus</u>, in fact, has enjoyed high status as an essential component of modern narrative. Ian Watt's study of the early practitioners of the genre prompted him to observe that attention to characterization is an element that definitively separates the novel from its sister genres, and from its fictional predecessors: "the novel is surely distinguished from other genres and from previous forms of fiction by the amount of attention it habitually accords...to the individualization of its characters..."[2]

Throughout the nineteenth century, the great Age of the Novel, character portrayal remained a dominant element of

1

fictional narrative. In the era of protagonists such as Emma Bovary, Raskolnikov, and Anna Karenina, detailed, lifelike characterization was obligatory. The development of stream-of-consciousness techniques late in the century, and the subsequent influence of Freud, added the unprobed depths of the individual psyche to the novelist's store of resources for depicting protagonists. Internal exploration of character has been fruitfully and exhaustively explored by Proust, Joyce, Faulkner, and others.

Critical pronouncements of the early twentieth century attest to the power and significance of the role of character in fiction. Henry James ignored Aristotle and equated character with action: "Character in any sense that we can get at it, is action, and action is plot."[3] For James' follower, Percy Lubbock, the capable novelist is one who draws characters of flesh and blood: "Of Richardson and Tolstoy and Flaubert we can say at once that their command of life, their grasp of character, their knowledge of human affections and manner, had a certain range and strength and depth."[4] In the concluding pages of Mimesis, Erich Auerbach praises Tolstoy and Dostoyevsky primarily for their ability to depict character: "The most essential characteristic of the inner movement documented in Russian realism is the unqualified, unlimited and passionate intensity of experience in the characters portrayed."[5]

By mid-twentieth century, successful narrative technique had become nearly synonymous with successful character portrayal. Leon Surmelian's <u>Techniques of Fiction Writing</u>, for example, declares that "Character is the cornerstone of the novel, and we read novels primarily for their revelations of character."[6] Gilbert Chase prefaces <u>The American Novel and Its Tradition</u> with the accepted observation that in fiction, "Character is more important than action and plot...."[7]

Despite these assertions, a growing reaction to the preeminence of character developed. While Joyce and Proust labored to plumb the depths of the human psyche, and thus merge <u>homo fictus</u> with <u>homo sapiens</u>, Einstein was positing the total relativity of our perception of "reality." In the new physics, "absolute description of any object or area is impossible from a single point of reference. Each position which provides a perspective will reveal a different aspect of the subject of observation and contemplation..."[8]

In 1939, Jean Paul Sartre related this concept to fiction. In his essay, "M. François Mauriac et la liberté,"[9] Sarte mocks the feigned "lucidité divine du romancier"(44) who attempts to assume "le point de vue de Dieu sur ses personnages" (45). For the French thinker, philosophic and scientific relativism must be reflected in the novel: "la théorie de la relativité s'applique intégralmente à la univers romanesque, que, dans un vrai roman, pas plus que le mond d'Einstein, il n'y a de place pour un observateur privilégie" (56-57). For many writers, the uncertainties of the modern age were mirrored in the increasingly denatured characters that their works depicted. Kafka's K, Beckett's Molloy, and Maurice Blanchot's Thomas l'obscur are stunted caricatures of their nineteenth-century counterparts.

Critics of fiction were quick to recognize the winds of change. José Ortega y Gasset lamented the dehumanization of art in general and of the novel in particular: "Por todas partes salimos a lo mismo: Huída de la persona humana...Es muy difícil que a un contemporáneo menor de treinta años le interese un libro donde, so pretexto de arte, se le refieran las idas y venidas de unos hombres y mujeres.[10] Alain Robbe-Grillet, in contrast, celebrates the demise of the novel of character:

...les créateurs de personnages, au sens traditionnel ne reússissent plus à nous proponer que de fantoches auxquels eux-mêmes ont cessé de croire. Le roman de personnages appartient bel et bien au passé, il caractérise une epoque: Celle que marquel'apogée de l'individu.[11]

The Formalist-Structuralist school of criticism has carried the concept of the denatured character to its logical extreme. Seymour Chatman notes that Vladimir Propp, in his seminal study, The Morphology of the Russian Folktale, viewed prototypical fictional characters as "simply the products of their functions in narratives."[12]   Aristotle, in the <u>Poetics</u>, had posited the possibility of a drama without characters: "Without action there could be no tragedy, whereas a tragedy without characterization is possible."[13]   Boris Tomachevski applied the Aristotelian argument to fictional narrative: "Le héros n'est guère nécessaire à la fable.   La fable comme système de motifs peut entièrement se passer du héroes et de ses traits caractéristiques."[14]

In 1964,   Claude Bremond proposed "the extension of the findings of Propp to literary and artistic genres other than the fairy tale" (Chatman 59).   The Structuralist conception of character in the novel is epitomized in the theories of A. J. Greimas.   In <u>Sématique structurale</u>,[15] he classifies characters not according to what they are, but according to what they do.   To this end, he even divests character of its traditional name, preferring to refer to fictional personages as "<u>actants</u>".   Most Structuralists agreed with this strategy, and perceived in the idea of character, "una peligrosa y desviada idea nacida por comodidad mental del lector y del crítico, un modo de referencia que oculta el verdadero mecanismo de su inserción en el relato."[16]

In part, the Formalist-Structuralist argument represented a reaction to traditional criticism's insistence that the novelist's principle task is the creation of flesh and blood characters that rival their parallels in the real world.   Belief in the extremes of such criteria frequently resulted in the degeneration of the

5

critical activity into a series of commentaries in which the focus moves from the work itself to the subjective fringe. L. C. Knights has illuminated the pitfalls of the application of such require- ments to the study of dramatic character in the aptly entitled essay, "How Many Children Had Lady Macbeth?"[17]

While traditional criticism occasionally breaks down into such idle speculation, its antithetical alternative, the Formalist- Structuralist method, is equally flawed by its rigid reductionism. In his lucid essay on the subject, Seymour Chatman concludes that "Literary analysis is so much more than the fitting of units into categories that we must question whether any desire to develop elaborate systems genuinely contributes to a clearer understanding of the literary work of art " (78). Today there is a manifest need for a critical approach to character that can retain an interest in the motivations of protagonists while drawing on the experience of the system builders. Northrup Frye's "Theory of Modes,"[18] although essentially dependent upon Aristotelian notions of character,[19] is an intelligent example of the potentialities of this process. Elsewhere, a critical precedent was established through the utilization of a Latin American text as the basis for a theoretical analysis of character. Floyd Merrel's essay, "Communication and Paradox in Carlos Fuentes' La muerte de Artemio Cruz: Towards a Semiotics of Character,"[20] seeks to show that the choices that a character makes within a

6

work of fiction ultimately lead to paradoxes on a semantic and existential level. When viewed experimentally and from multiple critical perspectives, the traditional vantage point of character thus may provide fresh insights to textual analysis and contribute as well to the concept of a poetics of fiction.

The narrative works of Mario Vargas Llosa lend themselves particularly well to studies of this nature. His extensive literary production offers an ample body of material for investigation. Twenty-eight years after the publication of his first novel, he remains in the vanguard of major Latin American novelists. Among the myriad of technical experimentors who figure in the Latin American "Boom" and "post-Boom," perhaps none has been cited so frequently for a preoccupation with novelistic technique as has Vargas Llosa. This awareness of the role of structural experimentation, "su candente fe en los procedimientos técnicos y estéticos de la novela,"[21] is observed in his own critical studies, which range from general observations on novelistic technique, such as La novela,[22] to book-length studies on Flaubert[23] and García Márquez.[24] Vargas Llosa's narrative works continue to represent "uno de los nervios más vigorosos,"[25] of current Latin American fiction.

Early critical appraisals of Vargas' powers of characterization were largely uncomplimentary. Though few scholars devoted much time to close analysis, the prevailing view

7

was negative: "Sr. Vargas Llosa does not in fact attempt to delve too deeply into his characters or their relationships...his characters are often quite unconvincing."[26] Roslyn Frank, in her excellent study of the author's early works, concluded that in the portrayal of character, his narrative frequently displays an "opacidad inherente."[27] Referring to La ciudad y los perros, Luis A. Díez affirmed that "Few characters are delineated in any great depth."[28] Elsewhere, in a review of Pantaleón y las visitadoras, Martín Vilumara cited "lo inverosímil de la mayor parte de los personajes."[29] Luis Harss concluded that Vargas Llosa's narrative contains "no rounded characters."[30]

A few critics contested this view. Phillip Johnson found the protagonist of Conversación en la Catedral, Santiago Zavala, to be both "complex and multifaceted."[31] Alan Cheuse, commenting on the mythic dimension of Vargasllosan protagonists, asserted that the author's characters "survive in our memories (where all books finally live or die)."[32] More recent studies continue this trend. Both María Rodriguez-Lee's Juegos sicológicos en la narrativa de Mario Vargas Llosa (1984)[33] , and Roy C. Boland's Mario Vargas Llosa: Oedipus and the Papa State (1988)[34], represent well this revisionist attitude in their concentration on Vargas Llosa's portrayal of the interiority of his characters and their social interrelationships.

Although the essays that follow continue in the tradition of Boland and Rodriguez-Lee, the critical approaches employed are at once less specific and more eclectic. Various dimensions of characterizaton and its interaction with other narrative elements from Los jefes (1958) to ¿Quién mató a Palomino Molero? (1986)[35] are analyzed from different critical perspectives, including reader-response theory, archetypal criticism, point-of-view theories, semiotics, structuralism, and approaches that incorporate elements of developmental psychology, rhetoric, onomastics, and theories of the role of place in fiction. Ultimately, however, it is the rich and complex fountainhead of Mario Vargas Llosa's fictional universe that has served as my definitive critical guidepost.

R. A. Kerr
Rollins College

NOTES

[1]Aristotle, On Poetry and Style, trans. G. M. A. Grube, 11th ed. (New York: Bobbs Merrill Co., 1958) 14.
[2]Ian Watt, The Rise of the Novel, 8th ed. (Berkeley: U of California Press, 1974) 17-18.
[3]Henry James, "Anthony Trollope," in Theory of Fiction: Henry James, ed. James E. Miller (Lincoln: U of Nebraska Press, 1972): 22.
[4]Percy Lubbock, The Craft of Fiction, 11th ed. (New York: The Viking Press, 1973) 4-5.
[5]Erich Auerbach, Mimesis, trans. Willard Trask, 4th ed. (Princeton UP, 1974) 522-23.

[6]Leon Surmelian, Techniques of Fiction Writing (New York: Anchor Books, 1969) 140.

[7]Gilbert Chase, The American Novel and Its Tradition (New York: Doubleday 1957) 12.

[8]Sharon Spencer, Space, Time and Structure in the Modern Novel (New York: New York UP 1971) xvii.

[9]Jean Paul Sartre, "M. Françoise Mauriac et la liberté," in Situations I (Paris: Librarie Gallimard, 1947):36-57.

[10]José Ortega y Gasset, "La deshumanización del arte," Obras completas, III, 5th ed. (Madrid: Revista de Occidente, 1962): 372.

[11]Alaine Robbe-Grillet, Pour un nouveau roman (Paris: Editions de Minuit, 1963) 28.

[12]Seymour Chatman, "On the Formalist-Structuralist Theory of Character," Journal of Literary Semantics, 1 (1972): 55. See Vladimir Propp, The Morphology of the Russian Folktale, trans. Laurence Scott, 2nd ed. (Austin: U of Texas Press, 1968) 25-26.

[13]Aristotle, On Poetry and Style, 59.

[14]Boris Tomachevski, "Thematique," in Théorie de la litterature, ed. and trans. Tzvetan Todorov (Paris: Editions du Seuil, 1965) 296.

[15]A[lgirdas] J[ulien] Greimas, Sémantique structurale: Recherche de méthode (Paris: Librarie Larousse, 1966).

[16]Raúl Castagnino, 'Sentido' y estructura narrativa (Buenos Aires: Editorial Nova, 1975) 77.

[17]L. C. Knights, "How Many Children Had Lady Macbeth?," in Explorations (New York: George W. Stewart, 1947):15-54.

[18]Northrup Frye, "Historical Criticism: Theory of Modes," in Anatomy of Criticism, 3rd ed. (Princeton: Princeton UP 1973) 36-67.

[19]Frye's categories are determined solely on the basis of a character's power of action within a literary work.

[20]Floyd Merrel, "Communication and Paradox in Carlos Fuentes' La muerte de Artemio Cruz: Towards a Semiotics of Character," Semiótica, 18 (1976): 339-60.

[21]José Luis Martín, La narrativa de Vargas Llosa (Madrid: Editorial Gredos, 1974) 62.

[22]Mario Vargas Llosa, La novela (Montevieido: Fundación de Cultura Universitaria, 1968).

[23]Mario Vargas Llosa, La orgía perpetua: Flaubert y Madame Bovary (Madrid: Taurus Ediciones, 1975).

[24]Mario Vargas Llosa, Gabriel García Márquez: historia de un deicidio (Barcelona: Monte Avila Editores, 1971).

[25]Martín 40.

[26]"Crowds Without Power," London Times Literary Supplement, 22 Sept. 1966: 872.

[27]Roslyn Frank, "La visión narrativa de Mario Vargas Llosa en Los jefes, La ciudad y los perros y Los cachorros," Diss. U of Iowa, 1972, 136.

[28]Luis A. Díez, Mario Vargas Llosa's Pursuit of the Total Novel (Cuernavaca, México: Centro Intercultural de Documentación, 1970), C. 1. 48.

[29]Martín Vilumar, "Mario Vargas Llosa: Pantaleón y las visitadoras," Camp de L'Arpa, No. 9 (January, 1974): 39.

[30]Luis Harss, " A City Boy," Texas Studies in Literature and Languages, 19 (1977): 495-502.

[31]Phillip Johnson, "Vargas Llosa's Conversacieon en la Catedral: A Study of Frustration and Failure in Peru," Symposium, 30 (1976): 205.

[32]Alan Cheuse, " Mario Vargas Llosa and Conversación en la Catedral: The Question of Naturalism," Texas Studies in Literature and Languages, 19 (1977): 445-51.

[33]María Rodríguez-Lee, Juegos sicológicos en la narrativa de Mario Vargas Llosa (Miami: Ediciones Universal, 1984).

[34] Roy C. Boland, Mario Vargas Llosa: Oedipus and the Papa State (Madrid: Editorial Voz, 1988).

[35] The editions of Vargas Llosa's works employed in the essays in this study are as follows:

Los jefes (Lima: José Godard, 1968)
La ciudad y los perros (Barcelona: Seix-Barral, 1973)
La Casa Verde (Barcelona: Seix-Barral, 1969)
Los cachorros (Madrid: Editorial Lumen, 1974)
Conversación en la Catedral (Barcelona: Seix Barral, 1974)
Pantaleón y las visitadoras (Barcelona: Seix Barral, 1973)
La guerra del fin del mundo (Barcelona: Seix Barral, 1981)
Historia de Mayta (Barcelona: Seix Barral, 1985).
¿Quíen mató a Palomino Molero? (Barcelona: Seix Barral, 1986)
El hablador (Barcelona: Seix Barral, 1987).

Individual novel titles will be abbreviated after first references in each chapter.

11

Chapter One

The Janus Mask

Quién sabe si vivimos nada más que alrededor de las personas, aún aquellas que viven con nosotros años y años. -- Manuel Rojas, Hijo de ladrón

Many inhabitants of Mario Vargas Llosa's fictional universe are "bicephalous"[1] or "disjunctive"[2] creatures whose personalities complicate and complement the works in which they appear. Bonifacia in La Casa Verde, for example, is also la Selvática; don Fermin Zavala doubles as Bola de Oro in Conversación en la Catedral; Alberto Fernández becomes el Poeta at the Leoncio Prado Military Academy in La ciudad y los perros. While such figures alternatively have been considered assets, oddities, or liabilities[3] in the Peruvian novelist's narrative, the full scope and purpose of their presence has not been adequately explored.

Multi-faceted or metamorphosed figures play a significant role in Mario Vargas Llosa's early fiction. These characters, modern embodiments of Janus, have at least two distinct identities. Duality is manifested by the assumption of different names. Almost invariably, one name is a nickname. Among major characters, an apodo functions as a verbal camouflage that conceals a protagonist's identity from the reader or from other

12

characters. The use of nicknames or alternate means of identification permits the development of two apparently unrelated stories that move along distinct narrative planes within the text. The planes eventually merge, revealing previously unperceived characterological dimensions and relationships.

The hidden role that a character plays can go undetected by the reader, by other characters in the work, or by both characters and reader. The effect in each case is distinct.

In one of Vargas Llosa's early stories, "El desafío," from the collection Los jefes, it is the reader who is unaware of the dual identity of one of the protagonists, don Leonidas. He is presented as a mere observer of the event that forms the nucleus of the story, the knife duel between Justo and el Cojo. For reasons that are unknown to the reader, both participants question the presence of the old man at the event. Leonidas ignores this hostility, and ultimately witnesses the slaying of Justo by el Cojo. As Justo prepares to fight, Leonidas offers last-minute advice, closing with the command, "ya, vaya, pórtese como un hombre" (57). El Cojo, after seriously wounding Justo, pleads with don Leonidas to persuade the wounded man to concede. The old man's response seals Justo's fate: "¡Calla y pelea!--bramó Leonidas, sin vacilar" (64). In the last lines of the story, as Justo's friends carry his body home, the reason for don Leonidas'

13

mysterious interest in the dual is revealed: "No llore, viejo -- dijo León--. No he conocido a nadie tan valiente como su hijo. Se lo digo de veras" (65). The casual revelation that el viejo don Leonidas is the father of the slain Justo shifts the focus of the story from the action of the duel to the stoic figure of don Leonidas. As the story ends, the full impact of the significance of the old man's presence, his advice to Justo, and of his refusal to stop the deadly duel is communicated to the reader through the perception of the character in a previously unrelated role. The dual identity of Leonidas as observer and father qualifies him as "una de estas entidades solapadas...típicas de Vargas Llosa,"[4] and helps to give the story "un valor emotivo más intenso"[5]

In "El desafío," the reader ultimately realizes that the characters' awareness of the relationship between Leonidas and Justo contributes to their unease at his presence at the duel. In contrast, the cadets at the Leoncio Prado Military Academy in La ciudad y los perros knownothing of each other's status prior to their enrollment in the school. The reader, equally ignorant at the outset, begins to associate the retrospective sequences that take place in Lima with specific nicknamed cadets at the academy. The first flashback section of the novel, for example, reveals the name of its protagonist: "A veces, su madre lo atraía hacia ella murmurando: 'Richi, Ricardito'" (15). Later, this name is linked to the nickname of an academy student, el Esclavo, as the young

14

cadet confesses his complicity in a cheating scheme to Lieutenant Gamboa: "...el Esclavo está de pie, muy pálido y no parece sentir las risas de los demás. --Nombre--dice Gamboa. --Ricardo Arana" (55).

The second section of the novel that deals with the military academy provides the surname of another cadet: "Bajo la bufanda de lana que le regaló su madre, los labios de Alberto se mueven sin ruido" (17). In the next division of the chapter, he is associated with the Miraflores district of Lima: "La casa de Alberto es la tercera de la segunda cuadra de Diego Ferré" (29). Alberto the Mirafloran is then quickly associated with his Leoncio Prado nickname, El Poeta: "--Necesito cincuenta puntos de Química --dice Alberto, la boca llena de pasta de dientes--. ¿Cuánto? --Te jalarán, poeta...No tenemos el examen, no fuimos" (37).

At this point, the reader's knowledge begins to transcend that of the cadets at the academy. This superiority remains partial, however, for the reader, like the characters, is largely ignorant that the retrospective monologues of an anonymous figure in Part One of the novel are actually the reminiscences of a third cadet, Jaguar. The confirmation that the timid adolescent who courts Teresa at Lince is also the brutal cadet overlord of the Leoncio Prado Academy occurs only in the epilogue of the novel.

15

In the cases of Jaguar and Richi Arana, the past and present facets of their lives dovetail at crucial moments in their histories. In Part One, four chronologically arranged sections detail Richi's arrival in Lima from Chiclayo, his hatred of his father, and his growing distrust of his mother In Part Two, Richi's last retrospective scene reveals his desire to enter the Leoncio Prado Academy in order to free himself from the influence of his parents: "Sería formidable mamá, me gustaría mucho...Siempre te he dicho que quería ir interno" (185). This section, which completes the narration about Richi's home life, is placed strategically between one that reveals the wounding of El Esclavo during maneuvers, and one that confirms his death. Thus, as the reader pieces together the final segments of the Richi/el Esclavo puzzle, the stories coalesce, and the complete portrait of the youthful scapegoat emerges.

The present and past narrations that comprise Jaguar's history in the novel are merged in a similar, if slower-paced fashion. The limited number of flashback sequences that chronicle his youth in Part One helps to keep his identity obscure at this stage of the novel. In this way, the narrative focus is directed toward the figures of el Esclavo and el Poeta. In Part Two, however, after Jaguar is accused of the murder of Richi, nine narrative sequences detail his love for Teresa and his collusion with the petty thief, el Flaco Higueras. As in the case of

Richi/el Esclavo, the two sides of Jaguar's personality are linked at a moment of crisis for him in the novel. In the same scene in which the disillusioned cadet leaves the military academy forever, he is definitively revealed to the reader as the young thief of the Callao district who steals to provide his girlfriend Teresa with trinkets. Once again, two sides of a character merge at precisely the moment at which each side's portrait is completed. The Jaguar that the reader glimpses briefly in the final pages of the novel is neither the adolescent thief nor the Leoncio Prado bully, but a mature blend of both stages of his prior existence.

Alberto Fernández is the characterological median against which the figures of Richi and Jaguar are contrasted. Appropriately, his history, and that of the academy Poeta, do not merge at a climactic point in the development of the novel. Since Alberto and el Poeta are conformists who shun the dangerous or the unusual, their convergence, like their personalities, is associated with normalcy and convention.

In each case cited, ultimate recognition of each character is delayed by concealment of his dual personalities within separate narrative sequences in the novel. Six planes converge to three as the reader's knowledge of the figures of Richi, Alberto, and Jaguar increases. The ultimate comprehension of these protagonists is partially determined by the method in which their binomial natures are joined within the narrative structure. The weakness of character recognized in el Esclavo is reiterated in Richi's sequences, and prepares the reader for his early disappearance in the narration. Part of our perception of Jaguar as an enigmatic figure stems from his deliberately attenuated, ambiguous portrayal. Unlike the instances of el Esclavo and el Poeta, the inner thoughts of Jaguar's Leoncio Prado existence are withheld from the reader. Our knowledge of this figure as cadet Jaguar is limited to his words and actions, and to the comments that other members of the squad make about him. His alter-ego in Part One of the novel, the studious, timid suitor of Teresa, is unrecognizable as the brutal Jaguar. Only in Part Two of the work, after the death of el Esclavo, do the increasing number of sections that outline Jaguar's past life of crime reveal a figure who conceiveably resembles the bully of the academy. Viewed chronologically, the trajectory from innocent colegio student to petty thief and potential murderer is plausible. Nevertheless, the shuffled, asynchronous structuring of these sequences creates an ambiguity in the personality of the protagonist that is reiterated in his alternate denial and admission of guilt of Richi's murder. Our conception of Jaguar, then, as with el Esclavo, is based not only upon the information that the narrator reveals about him in the course of the novel, but upon how this information is presented. Much like the texts of Fielding discussed in Wolfgang

Iser's _The Implied Reader_, the text of _La ciudad_ "offers itself as an instrument by means of which the reader can make a number of discoveries for himself that will lead to a reliable sense of orientation."[6]

In addition to the utilization of the Janus mask figure as a method of character presentation and as a way of structuring our perception of such presentation, the technique mirrors thematic preoccupations in _La ciudad_. The duality reflected in the title of the novel is reintroduced in the binomial aspects of the three protagonists. Ultimately, the putative antithetical character pairings are viewed not as disparate halves, but as reflections of a single, clearly defined character:

> ...in Vargas Llosa's novels, a character's past eventually catches up, chronologically, with his simultaneously depicted present, and...his present eventually catches up with his simultaneously depicted future. It is then that we see what seemed to be two wholly different characters are not only the same one, but also that one was developing inevitably into the other. If a character has appeared to be two different people at two different periods of his life, there turn out to be some fairly deterministic causes for the transition. [7]

In like manner, the city and the academy, originally construed as opposing forces in the lives of the characters, are ultimately displayed as macrosmic and microcosmic representations of a single morally bankrupt society. The Leoncio Prado Academy, like the verbal camouflage of the characters, superficially masks, but essentially reflects the corrupt ethos of Lima and of Peruvian society in general.

La Casa Verde, Vargas Llosa's second novel, has been described as a work whose existence is based upon "algunas identidades ocultas."[8] As such, it provides numerous examples of the use of Janus Mask, or multiple personality characters. Don Anselmo, Bonifacia, and Lituma, three major figures in the work, have dual personalities. Although the temporal and spatial dislocations in the novel are more severe than those in La ciudad, clues in the narrative again help to associate seemingly disparate figures.

Don Anselmo, founder of the Casa Verde, transforms into el Arpista. His link with the musician is established early in the narration. In the segment that introduces his character, he is linked to a particular musical instrument: "A veces recorría con amigos las chicherías mangaches y terminaba siempre en casa de Angélica Mercedes, porque allí había un arpa y él era un arpista consumado, inimitable" (56). Even after the construction of his brothel, Anselmo's predilection for the harp continued: "Don Anselmo, dicen, recorría incansable las chicherías de los barrios, y aun las de pueblos vecinos en busca de artistas...Pero nunca arpistas, pues él tocaba ese instrumento y su arpa presidía, inconfundible, la música de la Casa Verde" (98).

Anselmo's abduction of the orphan Antonia brings about the downfall of the musically-inclined entrepreneur and the

20

destruction of the original Casa Verde. Gradually, he metamorphoses into the figure of el Arpista, who frequents the bars of la Mangachería, playing for food and drink: "Los mangaches hablaron de don Anselmo, pero a él le decían arpista, viejo" (241). Eventually the formerly vigorous brothel owner, now aged and nearly blind, forms a small band with the guitarrist, el Joven Alejandro, and the drummer, Bolas. Although Anselmo's transition is clearly and chronologically delineated for the reader in Book Three of the novel, other characters, like the members of the group los Inconquistables, are unaware of the details of his prior existence as the proprietor of the Casa Verde. The harpist deliberately conceals these matters from them, in effect, denying his previous existence: "no hubo ningún incendio, ninguna Casa Verde--afirmaba el arpista--. Invenciones de la gente, muchachos" (228). Here once again, as in La ciudad y los perros, the reader is privy to information that is denied to characters in the novel.

While Anselmo evolves slowly and comprehensibly into el Arpista, the merging figures of Bonifacia and la Selvática, and Lituma and el Sargento do not fuse in such a predictable fashion. Part of the concealment of their Janus mask identities stems from the multiple space and time locus of the narrative sequences in the novel. Anselmo becomes el Arpista in a single location, Piura. The stories of Bonifacia and el Sargento are linked to Santa María de Nieva, while those of la Selvática and Lituma are linked with Piura. Additionally, the reader is at first unaware that the stories of these figures are unraveling during different time periods: la Selvática and Lituma's tales unfold years after those of el Sargento and Bonifacia. Several clues suggest that these four characters are actually two. El Sargento's home town, Piura, for instance, is actually noted by one of the soldiers, el Oscuro. The town is also Lituma's home town: "Se nota que es usted piurano, mi Sargento--dijo el Oscuro--. Todos los de su tierra son unos sentimentales" (127). Lituma, in a conversation with los Inconquistables, refers to his presence in Santa María de Nieva, where Sargento's history begins: "--No hablo de Lima, sino de Santa María de Nieva--dijo Lituma--. Noches como la muerte, Mono, cuando estaba de guardia" (142). Lituma helps to form another link of his person to that of el Sargento in the description of his treatment while in jail. In this dialogue, he refers to his past, and mentions el Oscuro, a figure associated with el Sargento and with Santa María de Nieva: "..me trataban bien. El cabo Cárdenas me hacía dar más comida que a cualquiera. Fue subordinado mío en la selva, un zambo buena gente, le decíamos el Oscuro" (82).

Clues that link the characters of la Selvática and Bonifacia, in contrast, are more suggestive than explicit. Both Bonifacia and her mentors at the orphanage in Santa María de Nieva refer to her in terms that are reminiscent etymologically of her future nickname, la Selvática: "--Y después protestas cuando las madres te dicen salvaje, --dijo la Superiora--" (90); "--Ya sé, Madre, por esto te pido que reces por mí--dijo Bonifacia--. Es que esa noche me volví salvaje..." (86). Additionally, the nuns' servant is described as having green eyes (25; 47), an unusual color for an Indian. La Selvática, the prostitute at the Casa Verde in Piura, is likewise described as having green eyes (66; 247).

A link between the Piuran Lituma and the Indian Bonifacia of Santa María de Nieva is made early in the novel. Lituma celebrates the return to his home town by proposing a toast in honor of the nuns' servant from the jungle outpost: "Por Bonifacia--dijo Lituma. Y alzó la copa, despacio" (64). Although la Selvática is not introduced in the narrative until Book Two, the stage has been set early in Book One for her entrance as a whore in the Casa Verde. A dialogue between los Inconquistables reveals that Bonifacia, soon to be recognized by her exotic nickname, has become a prostitute (83-84).

These clues concerning the true identity of Lituma/el Sargento and Bonifacia/la Selvática lead the reader, by the end of Book Two, to posit a relationship between them. The suppositions, while apparently correct, lack the causal element that definitively proves the linkage. Somewhere between the four stories and the multiple temporal and spatial sequences lies the event that causes the merging of these personalities.

This matter is resolved in Book Three by don Anselmo. While readers tentatively have linked the two young male and female figures, they also have observed Anselmo's transformation into el Arpista at his daughter's brothel. Since the blind musician was present at an event that is obscure to both the Selvática and the reader (the Seminario-Lituma Russian roulette challenge), the green-eyed prostitute asks him to relate the details to her. As the musician recalls the event, the final pieces of this identity puzzle fit into place: el Sargento is revealed as Lituma; Bonifacia as la Selvática.

As in La ciudad, Vargas Llosa's narrative expertise is reflected in the manner in which he first fragments and then reunites the two sides of each of these Janus mask personalities. The tale of the tragic events that took place at Chunga's bar are scattered in four separate sequences in the one-hundred pages of Book Three of the novel. The final transformation of Anselmo to el Arpista also is detailed in four segments in the same section of the work. Only when the old man's metamorphosis is complete, that is, when he returns as el Arpista to his daughter's replica of the original Casa Verde, does he conclude the narration of the events that transform el Sargento into Lituma and Bonifacia into la Selvática. Appropriately, the old man's definitive change and

24

the young couple's final transformation follow each other sequentially and close the narrative in Book Three. The work is structured in such a way that, as one protagonist's Janus mask personality is revealed, that character in turn is in the act of revealing the merging sides of two other characters.

In Vargas Llosa's third novel, <u>Conversación en la Catedral</u> "Arrangement...of characters and events is the beauty of the book."[9]   The Janus mask technique is essential to the organization of character in the novel. As in the case of <u>La ciudad</u> and <u>Casa Verde</u>, a triad of characters, Santiago, Hortensia, and don Fermín are dual personality characters.

Santiago Zavala, a "personaje contradictorio,"[10] is the protagonist of the narrative. Part of his ambivalent nature stems from the fact that several characters, including himself, perceive him in different ways. Each manifestation is represented by a name or a nickname: "Like so many of Vargas Llosa's characters, Santiago operates within several distinct contexts. In each he is known by a different name."[11] Distinct names, in addition to helping illustrate how others view Santiago, also facilitate the "identification of the stages of his life."[12] As a young man, Zavala is known to his brother Chispas and to his sister, Tete, as <u>el supersabio</u>, because of his predilection for poetry and application in his studies. Fermín Zavala, Santiago's father, affectionately refers to his son by another mote, <u>el flaco</u>.

25

Santiago's entrance into the cholo world of San Marcos University is the beginning of a transition in his personality that culminates in his existence as a nondescript news reporter. This metamorphosis is accompanied by a moral and intellectual transformation from idealist to skeptic, from skeptic to apathetic bourgeois. Santiago's last verbal, mask, the diminutive Zavalita, represents the antithesis of his youthful apodo, el supersabio: "El diminutivo subraya sútilmente la incorporación de Santiago Zavala al círculo de la derrota, de que también forman parte otros periodistas amigos.."[13]

The apodo Zavalita also has a technical function: "es el señal de un desdoblamiento interior del personaje, que le permite sostener un soliloquio consigo mismo, 'extrañarse' de su propia apatía y recobrar su lucidez."[14] This creates a series of dramatic asides in which Santiago, relating his story to the former servant, Ambrosio Pardo, steps out of his role as narrator and assumes that of self-inquisitor. His reflections on his university career offer cogent examples of this process: "Había sido ese primer año, Zavalita, al ver que San Marcos era un burdel y no el paraíso que creías? (107); "¿Había sido ese segundo año, Zavalita, al ver que no bastaba aprender marxismo, que también hacía falta creer?" (117).

In the mature Santiago's four-hour conversation with his father's ex-chauffeur, Ambrosio Pardo, the former servant repeatedly uses the term niño to address Santiago. This vocative usage has multiple functions. Initially it clarifies Ambrosio's relationship to Santiago, for he had been the family chauffeur years before his chance meeting with the reporter at the Lima dog pound. Logically, then, Ambrosio still remembers and refers to Santiago as if he were a boy: "Parece mentira verlo hecho un hombre...Lo veo y no lo creo, niño" (23).

Additionally, niño represents "un signo de sumisión y respeto,"[15] reflecting Ambrosio's view of Santiago as a member of the upper class. As a technical device, the apodo serves as a verbal signal that helps the reader, adrift in a sea of dialogue, to identify the accompanying segment as one taking place at the Catedral bar between Santiago Zavala and Ambrosio Pardo.

The repeated nicknames flaco, supersabio, and niño acquire an ironic flavor as the narrative progresses. In the last conversation in the novel between Santiago and his brother Chispas, the older Zavala continues to refer to his brother as el flaco or or el supersabio: "Le dio una palmada, hola supersabio, y tomó posesión con risueña desenvoltura de los dos cuartitos...--Te has buscado la cuevita, ideal, flaco..." (653). Santiago, at this juncture, is neither a flaco nor a supersabio. The voracious student intellect now aspires to blander intellectual activities: "¿Qué darián en el Colina, en el Montecarlo, en el Marsano? Almorzaría, un capítulo de 'Contrapunto' que iría languideciendo y

27

lo llevaría en brazos hasta el sueño viscoso de la siesta, si dieran una policial como "Rififí, una cowboy como 'Río Grande'. Pero Ana tendría su dramón marcado en el periódico, qué me pasa hoy día" (16). The slimness that don Fermín associated with the intensity of his son's late-night studies also has been transformed by maturity and inactivity: "...caramba, Zavalita, te sientas y esa hinchazón en el saco. . .Piensa: dentro de poco seré barrigón" (16). At this point in the narrative, such nicknames become ironic, since they effectively contrast Santiago's early aspirations with the realities of his mature life.

Santiago's enigmatic nature is due partially to the aura of independence and distinctiveness that each facet of his personality appears to convey in the novel. The dual personalities of Fermín Zavala and Hortensia in contrast, are mutually dependant. Through Books One and Two Fermín appears as a staid, upper-class businessman: "es un señor respetable, con una esposa respetable y un hogar respetable."[16] Consequently, the revelation in Book Three of his other identity, that of the homosexual Bola de Oro, is as much of a shock to the reader as it is to Fermín's son, Santiago.

Unlike don Fermín, Hortensia, the mistress of the political boss Cayo Bermúdez, is mentioned only indirectly in Book One of Conversación. She emerges as Bermudez' and the prostitute Queta's sexual partner in Book Two. Only after her death is

28

Hortensia definitively linked with la Musa, through each figure's affiliation with Cayo Bermúdez. As the reporters and police investigators gather at the scene of la Musa's murder and comment on the victim's past, the reader establishes the link between the drug-addicted prostitute and don Cayo's mistress: "-- Fíjese .. donde vino a morir- -el oficial Ludovico Pantoja señaló el cuarto con misericordia--. Después de vivir tan a lo grande. . . -- Claro, hombre--Periquito casqueó los dedos y dio un codazo a Santiago--. Fue la querida de Cayo Bermúdez" (374-375).

Thus, much as in La ciudad and Casa Verde, a central event in the novel, a death or a murder, serves as a link between disparate halves of Janus mask characters.

Once the characterological connection is made, the narrative systematically provides further details that confirm and elaborate upon the existences of both the homosexual Fermín and the prostitute phase of Hortensia's life. In Book Three, Amalia, a maid, traces Hortensia's history from her abandonment by Cayo Bermúdez to her move to the Jesus Maria barrio where she is murdered. Ambrosio, the ex-chauffeur, details his forced homosexual relationship with his employer in Book Four of the novel, and thereby confirms the Bola de Oro facet of don Fermín Zavala's personality.

Although at first glance Fermín and Hortensia's similarity derives from their analogous dual-nature personalities, the connection is in fact even more intimate. Both the reader and Cayo Bermúdez are introduced to la Musa by don Fermín (150-151). Subsequent commentary on la Musa's lesbianism by the elder Zavala also establishes a link between her and Hortensia, while arousing the interest of Cayo. La Musa, through her death, is indirectly responsible for the revelation to Santiago that his father Fermín also wears another mask, that of Bola de Oro.

The convergence of these four characters into two sheds light on the "dato escondido mayor,"[17] of the novel, the concealed connection between don Fermín, Ambrosio Pardo, and la Musa. The seeds of this mystery are sown early in Book One. Santiago Zavala interrupts his conversation with Ambrosio at the Catedral bar to demand an answer to a specific question that is as yet insignificant to the reader: "Que dejes de hacerte el cojudo. . .Que hablemos con franqueza de la Musa, de mi papá. ¿Él te mandó? Ya no importa, quiero saber. ¿Fue mi papá?" (29). The mystery of this implied relationship is compounded by the periodic appearance in the narrative of Book One of portions of a conversation between Ambrosio and don Fermín. These fragments make repeated reference to a deed performed by Ambrosio for don Fermín. In Book Three, as the prostitute Queta accuses Ambrosio of Hortensia/la Musa's murder, the significance of this information becomes apparent. "--Bola de Oro la mandó matar -- dijo Queta--. El matón es su cachero. Se llama Ambrosio ...

Hortensia le sacaba plata, lo amenazaba con su mujer, con contar por calles y plazas la historia de su chófer. . .No es mentira. En vez de pagarle a Hortensia. . .la mandó matar con su cachero" (395). The importance of don Fermín and Hortensia as Janus Mask characters, therefore, transcends their resemblance to similarly depicted characters created by the novelist. Because of their dual natures, the plot of the novel becomes dependent upon an aspect of character portrayal for its development. The fact that Fermín has a second side to his personality eventually causes la Musa's death. The murder, hinted at in Book One, and submerged in Book Two, resurfaces in Book Three as a prime focus of attention in the story. Introduced at the mid-point of the novel, it infuses new interest in the plot and sustains it until the end of the narration. Character duality and its consequences are thus responsible for the generation of an incident that stands at the center of the narration. The murder clarifies narrative references prior to it and prepares the reader for the explanations that follow. Conversación thus represents a high point in the utilization of Janus mask characterization in Vargas Llosa's narrative. Alongside the multi-faceted Santiago Zavala stand the opaque dualities of Fermín and Hortensia, whose binomial natures contribute to structure and plot while reiterating the ambiguity of human personality.

The use of Janus mask, or dual personality characters is grounded in the traditional concept of recognition. Aristotelian anagnorisis, or recognition, is defined in the Poetics as "a change from ignorance to knowledge of a bond....between persons."[18] In Greek Tragedy, the discovery takes place between protagonists in the play. Properly executed, it evokes an emotional response of pity or fear in the spectator. In Mario Vargas Llosa's early narrative, the change from ignorance to knowledge arises from the discovery that characters conceived of initially as separate individuals are actually facets of a single personality. The disclosure can take place between characters in a novel, or, as is more frequently the case, by the reader, who recognizes the bond that merges two figures in the story. At times, both reader and character discover the facts together; at times one possesses more information than the other. Reader awareness and character ignorance create dramatic irony; reader ignorance keeps him "in the same boat as the characters, and makes him share with the characters the complexities of the present moment."[19] In this approach to anagnorisis, the reader becomes an intellectual participant in the recognition process instead of an emotional respondent to it. Character becomes an important factor in the "engagement" by the reader by sharpening interest and personal involvement in the narrative through a process of remembering and recognition.

Dual personality characters are familiar figures in Vargas Llosa's fiction.[20] Facets of their natures are frequently unknown to the reader, to other protagonists, or to both reader and protagonists. Reader recognition often occurs during a climactic moment in the development of the character and at an important point in the structural organization of the work. The subsequent merging of narrative planes contributes to plot development and creates dramatic irony. The Janus mask technique denies the reader the usual complacency afforded by traditional techniques of character portrayal. Coincidentally, it entices the reader, urging participation in the novel, not from the vantage point of authorial omniscience, but from the limited perspective of the characters in the work.

NOTES

[1]Luis A. Diez, Mario Vargas Llosa's Pursuit of the Total Novel (Cuernavaca: Centro Intercultural de Documentación, 1970) C.1, 51.

[2] Carlos Fuentes, "El afán totalizante de Vargas Llosa," in La nueva novela hispanoamericana (Mexico, D.F.: Joaquín Mortiz, 1969) 36.

[3]David P. Gallager, in Modern Latin American Literature (New York: Oxford UP, 1973), Chapter 9, considers the dual personality figures in a positive light. Washington Delgado's review of La ciudad y los perros, in Letras, Año 37, No. 72-73 (1964): 310-15, considers this type character "non-realistic".

[4]José Miguel Oviedo, Mario Vargas Llosa: la invención de una realidad, 2nd ed. (Barcelona: Barral Editores, 1977) 87.

[5]Oviedo 87. A similar use of this technique is noted in the story ¡Diles que no me maten!" by the Mexican writer Juan Rulfo.

[6]Wolfgang Iser, The Implied Reader (Baltimore: The Johns Hopkins UP, 1974) 45.

[7]Gallagher 134.

[8] Emir Rodriguez Monegal, "Madurez de Vargas Llosa," _Mundo Nuevo_, No. 3 (Sept. 1966):71.

[9]Ronald Christ, "The New Latin American Novel," _Partisan Review_, 42 (1975):461.

[10]Alfredo Matilla Rivas, "_Conversación en la Catedral_," in _Homenaje a Mario Vargas Llosa_, ed. Helmy F. Giacoman and José Miguel Oviedo (New York: Las Américas, 1971) 89.

[11] Phillip Johnson, "Vargas Llosa's _Conversación en la Catedral_ : A Study of Frustration and Failure in Peru," _Symposium_, 30 (1976) 206.

[12] Johnson, 206.

[13] Hernán Loyola, "Vargas Llosa: _Conversación en la Catedral_, in _Homenaje_ 235.

[14] Oviedo 254.

[15] Oviedo 249.

[16] Oviedo 228.

[17] Matilla Rivas 72.

[18] Aristotle, _On Poetry and Style_, trans. G. Grube (New York: Bobbs Merrill, 1958) 21-22.

[19] Gallagher 129.

[20] See, for example, _La tía Julia_, where the character Lituma progressively assumes numerous identities, and Saúl Zaratas, alias _Mascarita_, who metamorphoses into an Indian storyteller in _El hablador_.

Chapter Two

The Secret Self

All narrative has a minimal pair of essential characteristics: "the presence of a story and a story teller".[1] Narrators assume diverse voices and perspectives in telling their tales. A useful distinction in this regard is between narration in which the narrator is present as a character, and that in which the narrator is absent from the tale.[2] When a protagonist narrates a portion of a work of fiction, part of our notion of his character arises from the perception of him in the role of storyteller. Analysis of a fictive narrator's comments may reveal aspects of the character's personality that remain hidden in the accounts of his actions in the novel.

Mario Vargas Llosa's first novel, La ciudad y los perros, has been described as a work in which "Few characters are delineated in any great depth."[3] Nevertheless, two figures, Jaguar and Boa, reveal much about themselves in their roles as narrators in the novel. Their commentaries, comprising about twenty percent of the work, provide refracted yet substantive self-portraits. In the wealth of critical studies devoted to the novel, the figure of Boa generally has been neglected. A review of the statements that he makes as storyteller reveals a characterologic complexity and diversity that merit critical consideration.

Boa Valdevieso narrates thirteen segments of the novel. Initially his monologues provide the reader with scabrous but factual generalizations about cadet life at the Leoncio Prado Military Academy. In detailing specific incidents, such as Cava's abortive attempt to steal a chemistry exam, and Richi's death while on manoeuvers, Boa's visceral reactions serve as an emotional barometer that reflects his function as "una directa emanación de la masa colegial."[4] Valdevieso's disparate narrations thus reveal a careful structuring that combines generality with specificity in a cohesive story unit.

In addition to contributing significantly to plot development, Boa's monologues reveal much about the teller of the tale. At the novel's outset, he is described from outside the frame of his own narration: "un cuerpo y una voz desmesurados, un plumero de pelos grasientos que corona una cabeza prominente, un rostro diminutivo..."(11). Later he is observed in action as a potential buyer of Alberto's pornographic novelettes, and as the lone defender of the beleaguered Jaguar. Almost everything else that the reader learns about his character is gleaned from his own narrative.

For his peers, Boa is epitomized in a word: "bruto" (20; 24l). This characterization is corroborated partially by his own testimony. He himself recalls participating in an incident in which cadet Cava rapes and kills a chicken. Later, he confirms his attempt to aid his companions in the sexual assault of a cadet, and reveals that he deliberately broke the leg of his dog.

Boa's worship of the machismo code represents another facet of his brutish nature. Although he fears and at times hates Jaguar, he admires him as "un hombre de pelo en pecho" (142). He glories in exertion that causes him to perspire heavily, since "así transpiran los machos" (68). Commenting on the exasperated weeping of his French instructor, Fontana, he reveals that for him, the shedding of tears implies effeminacy: "Y entonces cerró los ojos y cuando los abrió lloraba. Es un marica" (149). In contrast, instructors who respond forcefully to students, such as Lieutenant Gamboa, are viewed distinctly. After enduring harsh physical punishment ordered by the Lieutenant, the cadet's impression of the officer differs markedly from his view of Fontana: "Gamboa es formidable, ahí nos dimos cuenta de lo formidable que es Gamboa" (149).

Boa's racist commentaries reveal another aspect of his churlish nature. As a cholo, he views Whites with scorn: "Los blanquiñosos son pura pinta, cara de hombre y alma de mujer, les falta temple" (229). The serranos, Indian mountain peasants, receive even greater abuse. His comments on their attributes form a litany of ignorance and prejudice:

Los serranos son tercos...Los serranos son un poco brutos (l48);

Yo creo que el colegio le contagió las pulgas a la perra, las pulgas de los serranos...(179);

Los serranos son bien hipócritas....(l99)

The cruelty, machismo, and racism that Boa's own musings verify as aspects of his nature appear to paint a sordid portrait of a sadistic personality. Nevertheless, the cadet's own words reveal another side of his character, one that contrasts with, and to some extent ameliorates the brutish element. His cruelty, for example, is mitigated by his ingenuous, puerile nature. In this respect, his narrative has been compared to that of "la voz primaria y anormal del Benjy de The Sound and the Fury "(Oviedo 121). Symptomatic of his naïeveté is a fear of spirits and goblins. When plans go awry, he rationalizes that "El diablo se mete siempre en todo con sus cachos peludos" (7l). He believes that his dog can protect him from ghosts: "me hubiera gustado tenerla a mi lado en la glorieta, para espantar el miedo: ladra perra, zape a los malos espíritus" (247). Additionally, he associates Jaguar's features with a devil: "El diablo debe tener la cara del Jaguar, su misma risa y además los cachos puntiagudos" (14l). When causal explanations are lacking, the cadet's reaction is one of superstitious fatalism: "Estaba visto que nadie se salvaba, ha sido cosa de brujería" (265).

Such childlike superstitutions and fears are those of an immature or underdeveloped mind that does not always act according to logic or reason. Viewed in this light, Boa's demonstrations of brutality assume a different dimension. He rarely commits premediated acts of violence; rather, they result from anger, frustration, or from attempts to please other cadets. During the aforementioned attempted rape of a cadet, for example, Boa's monologue reveals that the incident was initiated by Jaguar, Rulos, and Cava. His role, though not laudatory, was limited to the physical restrainment of the victim.

Although he participates in the humilliation of Professor Fontana, his monologues reveal that Jaguar and Cava were the major instigators of these incidents. Boa expresses satisfaction at the baiting, yet feels compassion for the victim: "A veces da compasión, no es mala gente, sólo un poco raro... Es un buen tipo" (148-49).

When he actively participates in violence, such as the maiming of his pet, Boa accepts responsibility for his actions: "Le di la mala, con intención" (187). He likewise expresses sincere regret for his deed: "Es un animal bien leal, me compadezco de haberla machucado" (187).

Valdevieso's prejudice against serranos, outlined above, stems from impressions gained by witnessing the results of a beating inflicted upon his step-brother by Indians: "Será por eso que los serranos siempre me han caído atravesados" (20l). Despite an inculcated hatred, Boa comes to respect el serrano Cava as a friend. Boa, the oaf presumed idiot, is conscious of this radical change in attitude, and chronicles it in his monologue: "Pobre serrano, no era mala gente, después nos llevamos bien. Al principio me caía mal, por las cosas que le hicieron al Ricardo [su hermanastro]" (202). Ultimately, the cholo proposes friendship to the Indian: "Y después yo fui hasta la cama del pobre Cava y le dije: 'oye, quedamos como amigos.' Y él me dijo: 'por supuesto'" (204). At this juncture, the brutish cadet transcends his base nature, forming a bond of human affection based upon personal experience rather than on untested stereotypes.

Like many characters in La ciudad, Boa is not what he appears to be at first glance. His peers view him as a brute whose strength and atavistic cruelty are to be feared, respected, or exploited. Were it not for his monologues, Boa's second self would remain as hidden from the reader as it is from the academy cadets. As a narrator who ostensibly directs his comments only to himself or to his dog, he reveals that he can act responsibly and demonstrate affection. Dramatic irony is achieved through the reader's dual perception of Boa's façade together with a glimpse of the isolated cadet who loves his scraggly pet and who remains loyal to Jaguar and Cava.

Prior to its publication, one of the tentative titles proposed for La ciudad y los perros was Los impostores. While Boa's narrative provides essential information with regard to plot, the revelation of aspects of the cadet's own personality that surface in his narration also verifies his need to conceal his inner feelings, his hidden self, and to become yet another imposter in the savage environment of the Leoncio Prado Academy.

NOTES

[1] Robert Scholes and Robert Kellogg, The Nature of Narrative, 3rd ed. (New York: Oxford Univ. Press, 1971) 4.

[2] Gérard Genette, "Discours du récit," Figures III (Paris: Editions du Seuil, 1972): 252. Genette's terms are, respectively, récit homodiégétique and récit hétérodiégétique.

[3] Luis A. Díez, Mario Vargas Llosa's Pursuit of the Total Novel (Cuernavaca: Centro Intercultural de Documentación, 1970), C. I. 48.

[4] José Miguel Oviedo, Mario Vargas Llosa: la invención de una realidad, 2nd ed. (Barcelona: Barral Editores, 1977) 121.

Chapter Three

Narrators and Narratees

On le sait, dans la communication linguistique, je et tu sont absolument présupposés l'un par l'autre; de la même façon, il ne peut y avoir de récit sans narrateur et sans auditeur.
--Roland Barthes, "Introduction à l'analyse structural des recits"

All narrative art has a minimal pair of essential characteristics: the presence of a story and a story teller."[1] Historically, narrators have assumed diverse voices and perspectives in telling their tales. Careful study of the ways in which a story may be related did not begin, however, until this century. Henry James pioneered these investigations. In his Prefaces,[2] James identified and vilified the traditional use of omniscient or obtrusive narrators who are present in works such as Tom Jones and War and Peace. He preferred and prescribed a third person "center of consciousness" narrator who assumed the perspective of a "character who is inside the frame of the action rather than that of a disembodied presence who addresses the reader from outside the action."[3] James' third person reflector, as Wayne Booth points out, represents only "one mode among many."[4] Multiple narrative viewpoints, and first and second person narrators of questionable reliability, distance, and involvement have become commonplace in the modern novel.

In contradistinction to James, contemporary critics seek to emphasize the function and importance of the various narrative postures instead of prescribing specific methods of narration.[5] Gérard Genette, for example, makes a useful distinction between narrative homodiégétique, in which the narrator is present as a character, and narrative hétérodiégétique, in which the narrator is absent from the tale.[6] When a protagonist narrates a work of fiction, part of our notion of his character arises from the perception of him in the role of storyteller. His source of information, the degree of its objectivity and precision, and the sentiments that the story arouses in him need to be taken into consideration when the effect of the narration is determined. Clearly, this effect is related to the reader's overall conception of the character who tells the tale. In the novel, as in life, what we come to believe is partially conditioned by our estimation of the conveyors of the information that we receive.

All narratives require a teller and a tale. Additionally, some critics[7] now realize the potential significance of the listener of a story: "Any narrative presupposes not only a narrator, but also a 'narratee,' the receiver of the narrator's message."[8] Narrative receptors may be classified in the same manner as the story's emittors, that is, "according to their degree

43

of involvement in the events recounted in the narrative."[9] Such categories range from a non-involved, unspecified narratee to a character who knows and has participated in the incidents that the story relates. When the narratee is a protagonist in the novel, the reader's conception of his role as auditor is conditioned by the knowledge of him as a character.[10]

Although Mario Vargas Llosa does not limit his narrative strategy to the use of characters as emittors and receivers, his persistent recourse to this approach[11] represents a significant and overlooked area in the study of his literary production. In Conversación en la Catedral, for example, the role of character narrators and narratees is quintessential. The frame of the novel is a conversation in a bar, la Catedral, between Santiago Zavala, a Lima reporter, and Ambrosio Pardo, the former chauffeur of don Fermín Zavala, Santiago's deceased father. As Ambrosio and Santiago converse, their words evoke other characters, prior actions, and dialogues. In this manner the novel's temporal and spatial focus expands from a four-hour conversation in Lima to an extended chronicle of recent Peruvian history.

The catalytic Santiago-Ambrosio Conversation is not a true dialogue, for it soon breaks down into each protagonist's "separate recollections,"[12] that are scattered throughout the novel. Ambrosio and Santiago become more than interlocutors in a dialogue: they are both narrators, and at times, narratees.

In the course of Conversación, the young Zavala relates parts of his history to Ambrosio at the Catedral, and portions to his friend Carlitos at the Negro-Negro bar. Reflecting on his past, he creates a third, inner narration in which he is both narrator and narratee. Ambrosio details portions of his life to Santiago, to a prostitute, Queta, and to Zavala's father, don Fermín.

In addition to their informational value, Santiago's narratives project three distinct images of his personality. The laconic mask that he shows to Ambrosio, the cynical image that he conveys to Carlitos, and the guilt-ridden self-portrait that surfaces in his inner monologues are actually facets of a single, complex personality.

Throughout the narration to Ambrosio, Santiago maintains a mattter-of-fact posture that belies his inner turmoil. He relates family details, such as the marriage of his sister, la Tete, his involvement with a young radical, and his father's death, in a detached, business-like way:

--[La Tete] Se casó con ese muchacho que iba a la casa --dice Santiago--. Popeye Arévalo. El pecoso Arévalo (35);

--[Me enamoré de] Una compañera de San Marcos --dice Santiago-- Hablaba de política, creía en la Revolución (76);

--Pero no fue esa vez --dice Santiago--. [Mi padre] Murió al segundo ataque, Ambrosio. Un año y medio después. (530)

45

The objective tone of these observations is transferred to Santiago's assessment of himself and others. He describes his impression of his deceased father with cold efficiency: "A mí no me parecía gran hombre, sino una canalla" (180). A self-deprecating summary of his own personality conveys a similar aura of precision and distance: "... soy como esos animales que ante el peligro se encogen y quedan quietos esperando que los pisen o les corten la cabeza ...." (123). In the rare instance in which Santiago admits to an emotion, he appends a qualifying statement that reduces its affective impact. When the ex-chauffeur inquires if he is happily married, for example, Zavala declares: "Sí estoy ... lo que pasa es que ni eso lo decidí realmente yo. Se me impuso solo, como el trabajo, como todas las cosas que me han pasado. No las he hecho por mí. Ellas me hicieron a mí más bien" (542). Santiago's emotional estrangement and depersonallized commentary are reminiscent of Merseault's narrative in L'Étranger. Camus' clerk and Vargas Llosa's reporter relate important events of their own lives with the clinical detachment of outsiders.

The Santiago who regularly discusses his past with Carlitos at the Negro-Negro bar differs markedly from his counterpart at the Catedral. At the Negro-Negro, Zavala abandons his pose of objectivity and reveals emotion, anguish, and doubt. In recounting his disillusionment with a Communist youth group that he joined

46

while a student at San Marcos University, for example, he relates that "Era en medio de esas reuniones que de repente sentía que nunca sería un revolucionario, un militante de verdad ... De repente una angustia, un mareo, una sensación de estar malgastando el tiempo" (170). Zavala's sarcastic analysis of his own role as a news reporter, which he summarizes for Carlitos, contrasts with the negative yet unemotional self-portrait that he painted for Ambrosio: "Acumulando mierda con mucho enthusiasmo, hoy día un montoncito, mañana otro poquito, pasado un pocotón ... Hasta que hubo una montaña de mierda. Y ahora a comértela hasta la última gota, eso es lo que me pasó, Carlitos"(385).

A cogent, sustained example of Zavala's emotional involvement in his own narration to Carlitos appears in his eye-witness account of a confrontation between the political strongman Cayo Bermúdez, and his father don Fermín Zavala. After Santiago was arrested along with his Communist comrades, Fermín was forced to humble himself before the official in order to secure his son's release. Cayo and Fermín's evoked dialogue on this occasion is punctuated by Santiago's impressionistic classification of the participant's reactions and impressions. Don Fermín appeared to his son to react in many different ways:

--con amabilidad, Carlitos, como si lo lamentara--(207);

47

--con una furia frenada, Carlitos, sin alzar la voz, aguantándose las ganas de decirle perro, sirviente(208);

--sonriéndole, asintiéndo, Carlitos, tratando de demostrarle que ya se había reconciliado con él --.(209)

Cayo Bermúdez, according to the young reporter, countered with a series of equally theatric false postures:

--como escandalizado, Carlitos, de que no le entendieran las bromas-- (208);

--como si estuviera diciendo tonterías en una reunión social, Carlitos, como si le importara un comino lo que le decía--(207-208);

--compungido, Carlitos, queriendo renvindicarse, congraciarse-- .(209)

As Santiago interprets the motivations that lie behind Cayo and Fermin's words, he communicates the sense of shame, outrage, and cynicism that the incident provoked in himself.

Santiago assumes the role of dispassionate observer in narrating his story to Ambrosio. During his commentaries to Carlitos, he begins to reveal fragments of his own feelings about the incidents that he relates. Yet even Carlitos is not privy to the tangled web of thoughts and emotions that Santiago displays in his internal monologues. These segments, which are signalled by the key words piensa and Zavalita, comprise the reporter's third narration. They are unique in several ways. Of the trio of stories that he recounts, this group is the most extensive and frequent in occurrence. The monologues transcend the four-hour time span

48

that circumscribes the relation to Ambrosio and that nominally limits Santiago's statements to Carlitos. Zavala's "dialogue within consciousness,"[13] begins in the novel's first paragraph, prior to the encounter with his father's ex-chauffeur: "El era como el Perú, Zavalita, se había jodido en algún momento. Piensa: ¿en cuál?" (13). When the introspective narrative does occur within the primary four-hour frame it presents the possibility of a double perspective: "una dirigida hacia atrás, simultánea a los acontecimientos, y otra desde el tiempo de la enunciación."[14]

As the protective shield that controls Zavala's commentaries to Ambrosio and to Carlitos is lowered, new aspects of his personality emerge. These at times contradict the statements that he makes in his other narratives. Although he professed no love for his father to Ambrosio, for example, he does not hide his sympathy for the deceased don Fermín from himself: "Será tu culpa, Zavalita, pobre papa, pobre viejo"(24); "Piensa: pobre papá"(30). The self-deprecation and personal anguish that surface in the conversations with Carlitos intensify in Santiago's monologues:

... piensa: te sentiste torturado, exilado, traicionado, Zavalita... (84);

... conmovido, piensa, agradecido, Santiago les contaba sus peleas sobre la religión ... (87);

Ahí estaban los ojos burlones y estupefactos de Carlitos, Zavalita, ahí el malestar que sentías. (341)

The full impact that Zavala's life of doubts and indecision exerts on his personality is revealed only in the cold honesty of his self-reflective narrative:

Años que se confunden, Zavalita, mediocridad diurna y monotonía nocturna, cervezas, bulines. Reportajes,crónicas...Conversaciones en el Negro-Negro, domingos con chupe de camarones, vales en la cantina de la Crónica.. Borracheras sin convicción, Zavalita, polvos sin convicción, periodismo sin convicción .... (412)

Part of what we perceive as Santiago's personality arises from the distinct postures that he assumes in his narrations. Taken individually, the three tales represent a movement from an exterior of feigned detachment to the emotional core of his tortured personality. In the course of the novel, fragments of each type narration are often intertwined in order to present simultaneously the seemingly disparate aspects of the same personality. The result is a narration that succeeds in presenting a story while conveying the individual complexity of the teller of the tale.

Like Santiago, Ambrosio Pardo narrates three stories in Conversación. At the Catedral bar, he relates his fortunes to Zavalita. In the novel's narrative past, at the elder Zavala's retreat at Ancón, he recounts to don Fermín the details of his early life in the village of Chincha. In another past narration, the chauffeur relates to the prostitute Queta the events leading up to his seduction by his employer, don Fermín.

Unlike Santiago's comments, Ambrosio Pardo's narratives tend to reaffirm a simple, consistent personality rather than a complex, changeable one. Ambrosio reveals his apparently genuine compassion for others in all his narrations. Although his father, an ex-criminal, extorted money from him under threat of violence, the zambo still felt sympathy for him: "--No pena porque hubiera estado preso, entiéndame bien, niño --dice Ambrosio--. Sino porque parecía un pordiosero. Sin zapatos, unas uñotas de este tamaño, unas costras en los brazos y en la cara que no eran costras, sino mugre. Le hablo con franqueza, vea"(133-34). Years after leaving the town of Pucallpa, Ambrosio still expresses concern for his daughter, Amalita Hortensia, whom he left in the care of a neighbor, doña Lupe: "...yo también me paso los días acordándome de Amalita Hortensia --dice Ambrosio--. Pensando cómo será, a quién se parecerá" (113). In relating to don Fermín the history of Rosa, Cayo Bermúdez' abandoned wife, the chauffeur pauses to express pity for her plight: "Es verdad que la Rosa se puso indiota y se llenó de lunares, pero en el fondo su historia daba compasión, ¿no, don?" (70). Ambrosio's most impassioned statements of respect and sympathy are reserved for Fermín Zavala. Despite being regularly forced to submit to his employer's homosexual advances, he consistently defends Zavala

51

from Queta's continued diatribe: "No es un desgraciado, no es un déspota. Es un verdadero señor. Ya le he dicho" (628); "Yo sé cómo es. No es de los que insultan, no sabe tratar mal a la gente...Es un señor, no lo que usted cree" (631). Fermín's homosexuality, which earns him the nickname Bola de Oro in the bordellos of Lima, arouses sympathy rather than condemnation from his employee: "Es algo de dar pena...a mí me da, a él también...Si le viera la cara diría se le murió o alguien le han dicho que se va a morir esta noche" (628).

The irony that surrounds the figure of Ambrosio arises from the apparent disparity between the servile, compassionate narrator and the brutal murderer of la Musa, a drug-addicted prostitute and former mistress of Cayo Bermúdez, who threatens to reveal don Fermín's homosexuality. By slaying Cayo's ex-lover, Ambrosio carries his respect and sympathy for Fermín to absurd proportions. The murder becomes the supreme act of compassion for the man who sexually enslaves and humiliates him. In victimizing la Musa, Ambrosio himself becomes a victim: "Ambrosio ha alcanzado el punto máximo de la entrega: ha cargado con todas las culpas sacrificando su propia suerte ...."[15]

At the Catedral bar Ambrosio and Santiago are not only narrators. Since each listens to the other's recollections, they are also narratees. Both men are inquisitive listeners whose questions often determine the direction of the story that they hear. Ambrosio's question, "¿Por qué se escapó de la casa esa vez, niño?" (178), for example, results in the story of Santiago's Communist involvement and subsequent arrest. In Book One of the novel, Zavalita, seeking to clarify Ambrosio's statements concerning his stay at a mountain village, inquires, "¿Qué desgracia te pasó en Pucallpa?" (72). This query results in an extensive narrative in Book Four, in which the chauffeur outlines the events in his life that eventually prompted his return to Lima.

In general, Santiago's and Ambrosio's roles as auditors reinforce the character traits that they display as narrators. Zavala maintains his detached, objective pose by contributing matter-of-fact commentaries to Ambrosio's narrative: "--Tú conocías a mi papá mejor que yo --dice Santiago--"(115); "--Así que en Pucallpa y por culpa de ese Hilario Morales, así que sabes cuándo y por qué te jodiste --dice Santiago--"(74). Ambrosio reflects his compassionate nature by commiserating with Santiago over his frustrated love for Aída: "Usted quería enamorarla y no podía, teniendo ahí el otro --dice Ambrosio--. Sé lo que se siente siendo cerca de la mujer que uno quiere y no pudiendo hacer nada" (109). As Zavala relates the details of his father's death, Ambrosio reiterates his feeling for don Fermín: "siento un nudo aquí, niño...Un hombre como él no se debía morir" (531).

In the case of both Ambrosio and Santiago, however, momentary lapses make the reader aware of other sides of their narratee personalities. Zavalita's final questions to Ambrosio, questions that concern his father's possible role in the murder of la Musa, and that go unanswered, reveal the anger behind his pose of objectivity: "Que dejes de hacerte el cojudo --cierra los ojos, toma aire--. Que hablemos con franqueza de la Musa, de mi papá. ¿El te mandó? Ya no importa, quiero saber.¿Fue mi papá?"(29). The loyalty and sympathy that Ambrosio displays as narrator and narratee is undermined when he deliberately makes false observations about Santiago's narrative. As the reporter reveals his role in the investigation of la Musa's murder, the zambo nervously comments: "--Ni vi los periódicos ni sé de qué habla --dice Ambrosio--. Yo estaría en Pucallpa cuando eso, niño" (375). When Zavalita mentions the prostitute Queta, whom the chauffeur had visited frequently during the time period, Ambrosio reacts in a similar manner: "--¿Queta?--dice Ambrosio, y unos segundos después, atontado-- ¿Queta, niño?... --Nunca la oí, nunca la vi --dice Ambrosio--. A mí no me iba a hablar don Cayo de sus polillas, yo era su chófer, niño"(384).

Santiago's narrative monologues, by definition, represent an instance in which "the narrator does not direct his narration towards anyone but himself and is his own narratee."[16]As such, his personality traits as auditor duplicate those outlined above that he displays as narrator. In a few instances, the phrase "ay, Zavalita" that accompanies a narration provides a brief emotional commentary similar to that supplied by a commiserating narratee. As he ponders the options that are now unavailable to him, for example, the brief phrase heightens his own sense of despair over what might have been: "¿Te habrías recibido de abogado, casado, sido asesor de un sindicato, diputado, más desgraciado o lo mismo o más feliz? Piensa: ay, Zavalita" (161).

Other minor character-narratees in Conversación include don Fermín Zavala, Carlitos, the alcoholic reporter, and Queta, the prostitute. Late in the novel, Ambrosio reveals to Queta that Fermín was an inquisitive listener: "--Le cuento cosas de mí...De Chincha, de cuando era chico, de mi madre. De don Cayo, me hace que le cuente, me pregunta por todo" (629). Despite this assertion, Fermín never interrupts Ambrosio's narrative during the course of the novel. His presence is detected only through the vocative don, which Pardo regularly interjects in his story. Fermín's role as auditor remains nebulous until clarified by Queta. She suggests to Ambrosio that his employer's quiet eagerness to hear his narrative is a ploy calculated to ease the chauffeur's anxiety before having sexual relations with him: "--Te quita el miedo, te hace sentir cómodo --dijo Queta-- El gato con el ratón" (629). Fermín's silence is thus perceived as a calculated endeavor to mute the difference in social class between himself

55

and Ambrosio. Fermín's desire to manipulate his servile chauffeur thus emerges even through the calculated speechlessness of his role as auditor.

Like Santiago and Ambrosio, Carlitos and Queta are inquisitive narratees whose queries influence the content and direction of the stories that they hear. Additionally, their explicit commentaries on what they hear reveal their cynical, realistic natures. As a friend of Santiago, Carlitos assimilates more details of his friend's story than could the ex-servant, Ambrosio. Unlike the chauffeur, however, he reacts to the narration with sarcasm rather than sympathy: "Pareces una puta vieja que recuerda su juventud, Zavalita...Tú parece que hubieras dejado de vivir cuando tenías dieciocho años"(172).

As Ambrosio details his homosexual affairs with don Fermín, Queta responds with a disdain and disgust that approximates Carlitos' statements to Santiago: "A ti te gusta eso, ya me he dado cuenta. Ser el ratón. Que te pisen, que te traten mal" (611);

"--Tenías miedo porque eres un servil --dijo Queta con asco--. Porque él es blanco y tú no porque él es rico y tú no . Porque estás acostumbrado a que hagan contigo lo que quieran"(615).

The cynicism of Queta and Carlitos and their realistic appraisals of the stories that they listen to contrast sharply with Ambrosio's servility and Santiago's chronic indecision. As secondary figures whose personalities develop primarily through their roles as narratees, they form an effective counterpoise to their respective narrator's positions.

Character narrators and narratees abound in Conversación. In their alternating roles as tellers and listeners, protagonists impart their own interpretations to the narratives and commentaries, while revealing characterological dimensions that would otherwise be unperceived or unappreciated. No voice is authoritative; none is correct. All discussion conveys biased interpretations of information, and these interpretations mirror the personalities of the character narrator and character narratee. The richly intricate, and often deliberately ambiguous story is a reflection of the natures of its own tellers and listeners.

NOTES

[1] Robert Scholes and Robert Kellogg, The Nature of Narrative, 3rd ed. (New York: Oxford UP, 1971) 4.

[2] Henry James' Prefaces are collected in The Art of the Novel, ed. R. P. Blackmur (New York: Charles Scribner's Sons, 1934).

[3] Scholes and Kellogg 272.

[4] Wayne Booth, The Rhetoric of Fiction, l0th ed. (Chicago: U of Chicago Press, 1973) 153.

[5] See, for example, Norman Friedman, "Point of View in Fiction: The Development of a Critical Concept," PMLA, 70 (1955): 1160-84; Wayne Booth, Rhetoric of Fiction; Robert Scholes and Robert Kellogg, The Nature of Narrative; Gérard Genette, "Discours du récit," Figures III (Paris: Editions du Seuil, 1972):67-268.

[6] Genette 252.

[7]See ,for example, Tzvetan Todorov, "Les categories du récit litteraire," Communications, 8 (1966:146-47; and Roland Barthes, "Introduction à l'analyse structurale des récits," Communications, 8 (1966):18-19.

[8]Gerald Prince, "Notes Towards a Categorization of Fictional Narratees," Genre, 4 (1971): 100.

[9]Prince 100.

[10]William Faulkner's Absalom! Absalom! is a brilliant example of a work in which protagonists both narrate stories and respond to them as inquisitive narratees. See Hyatt Waggoner's study, "Past as Present: Absalom! Absalom!," in Faulkner: A Collection of Critical Essays, ed. Robert Penn Warren (Englewood Cliffs, N. J.: Prentice Hall, 1966): 175-85.

[11]Character narrators appear in Vargas Llosa's earliest stories and persist through El hablador (1987) Character narratees figure prominently in La Casa Verde (1966).

[12]Jean Franco, "Conversations and Confessions: Self and Character in The Fall and Conversation in the Cathedral," Texas Studies in Literature and Language, 19 (1977): 457.

[13]Franco 455.

[14] Casto M. Fernández, Aproximación formal a la novelística de Vargas Llosa (Madrid: Editoral Nacional, 1977) 41.

[15]José Miguel Oviedo, Mario Vargas Llosa: la invención de una realidad, 2nd ed. (Barcelona: Barral) 224.

[16] Prince 102.

Chapter Four

Modes of Characterization

Human beings do not live in a vacuum: "What is distinctly human comes from the primary fact that man lives his life in groups, with other people."[1] Fictional protagonists resemble real life figures in their social relations with other characters in a fictional universe. A character "interacts with other characters, who respond to him, in situations to which he responds, and his character is the impression thereby produced."[2]

Diverse strategies have been adopted for analyzing the relationship of character to society in Mario Vargas Llosa's narrative. Society itself has been classified as a protagonist.[3] Attempts have been made to organize characters, "ubicándolos en el juego de sus relaciones actanciales, como piezas del complicado mecanismo puesto en función por sus novelas."[4] Additionally, an effort has been made to formulate "reglas que rigen las acciones de los personajes."[5]

In reading any novel, "we are encouraged to make all sorts of provisional assessments, and provisional classifications; so we assemble characters in groups and classes."[6] Vargas Llosa's narrative offers a ready-made system of classification and assemblage that elucidates the treatment of character and society in his novels. Interpersonal communication takes place within a multitude of clearly defined and rigidly delineated groups, pandillas, or societal organizations. His novels often depict an entire network of interpersonal relationships, from the basic small group unit, the family, through child peer groups and adolescent and adult patotas, to full-fledged adult associations and institutions. Family and peer group nuclei figure prominently in works like La ciudad y los perros, Los cachorros, and La tía Julia y el escribidor. Institutionalized organizations, such as the military, religious and political groups, and prositute pandillas frequent the works that treat a broader social spectrum, such as Conversación en la Catedral, La Casa Verde, Pantaleón y las visitadoras, and La guerra del fin del mundo. The range of artistic focus thus flows from the observation of a single peer group to the kaleidascopic presentation of myriad groups and organizations that coalesce and overlap. Within this framework, patterns or modes of characterization recur.

One class of Vargasllosan protagonist may be termed the Outsider. Members of this category are aloof, enigmatic figures who shun conventional societal groups and are only peripherally influenced by them. Pedro Camacho in La tía Julia epitomizes the Outsider. Convinced of the artistic status of his work as a hack writer, he is rude, reclusive, and humorless. The escribidor is

60

incapable of true friendship and communication with others, since, "Para Pedro Camacho, no existía nadie fuera de él mismo" (191). Camacho's exalted sense of self-importance as a writer reaches a stage in which he believes that, "Si paro, el mundo se vendría abajo" (291).

Fushía and Anselmo, two figures from Casa Verde, are other Outsiders. Fushía's relationships with others arise either from necessity or greed. As a youth, he co-operates with two crooks in order to escape from jail only to betray them afterwards. He uses his lover, Lalita, either for his own sexual fulfillment, or as sexual bait for his enemy, Julio Reátegui. In his raiding parties, he assumes the role of patrón, giving orders and refusing to delegate authority. Even after his immobilization by advancing leprosy, he persistently tries to reject the assistance of the benevolent Aquilino: "Quién eres tú para mandarme--dijo [Fushía]... Es mi vida, Aquilino, no la tuya" (361). As a loner with no use for people other than in the service of his own advancement, Fushía proudly boasts, "¿Acaso no he traicionado a todo el mundo?" (31).

Don Anselmo is an equally solitary figure in Casa Verde. His behaviour after his arrival in Piura prompts the townspeople to nickname him "el extraño" (54). He rebuffs attempts at serious communication with others: "Él respondía con burlas y dichos ambiguous" (78); "don Anselmo replicaba con frases que parecían enigmas" (79). After the construction of the Casa Verde, Anselmo becomes even more reclusive: "Don Anselmo habitaba el último piso, esa angosta cúspide, y nadie, ni sus mejores clientes ... tenían acceso a ese lugar" (102). Symbolically, the only meaningful relationship that el extraño has with another person during this stage of his life is with one whose means of communication with the world have been cut: the blind, mute foundling, Toñita. Only after his metamorphosis as el Arpista does Anselmo succeed in establishing a continuing relationship with others as a member of La Orquesta.

Cayo Bermúdez, director del gobierno in Conversación, is another Vargasllosan Outsider. In the course of the novel, the reclusive Bermúdez abandons his wife Rosa and his mistress Hortensia, and is instrumental in the removal of his supporter, Colonel Espina, from the government. His sexual preference, voyeurism, symbolically dramatizes his detached, uncommitteed personality. Upon his ouster, Cayo's parting advice to his aid, Paredes, confirms this impression: "Te voy a dar un buen consejo... No te fíes ni de tu madre" (513).

In La guerra del fin del mundo, the societal Outsider is crystalized in the inscrutable figure of Antonio el Consejero, who mesmerizes the yaguncos while maintaining a personal emotional distance and aloofness. The successive military victories of the Canudos populace increasingly disengage Antonio from direct

62

contact with the majority of his followers, a distancing that is highlighted in the formation of inner sanctum groups such as el Coro Sagrado and la Guardia Católica, which insulate and isolate him from his disciples.

Outsiders, the black sheep in Vargas Llosa's fictional world, move along the fringes of society and its established institutions. All achieve a degree of success in their undertakings, but all ultimately are frustrated. Pedro Camacho's artistic snobbery leads to insanity. Fushía's boastful self-sufficiency is mocked in his helplessness at the leper colony. Solitary Anselmo's monomanic empire, symbolized by the Casa Verde, is burned to the ground. After the collapse of the Odría dictatorship in Conversación, Cayo Bermúdez, the Outsider, is forced into exile in Brazil. Antonio el Consejero dies after seeing Canudos reduced to rubble in La guerra. Outsiders shun normal social contacts. Appropriately, they find themselves isolated from such contacts after their fall.

Although the figure of the Outsider looms large in Vargas Llosa's fiction, many protagonists follow a different pattern. These individuals, termed Conformers, are assimilated in groups and institutions at various levels, and enjoy the advantages of the association. At some time in their fictional existence, however, most Conformers make moral or ideological stands that conflict with group standards or interests. The consequences of such

63

stands vary, depending upon external circumstances and the individual character's psychological make-up. Alberto Fernández in La ciudad is the archetypal Vargasllosan conventionalist: "One personality trait stands out throughout his life: his conformity."[7] The bourgeois concerns of his Miraflores pandilla, adolescent parties and ritualistic courtship ceremonies, contrast violently with the perverse order of the perros' social code at the Leoncio Prado academy. Alberto, chameleon-like, successfully adapts himself to his new group "by acting the part of a hard-boiled, dare-devil cynic."[8]

The murder of Richi Arana lights a spark in Alberto's conscience that prompts him, for once, to seek justice instead of conformity. By this time, however, expediency is too deeply ingrained in his personality to be uprooted by a single courageous act. When confronted with evidence of his career as the squadron pornographer, Alberto's initiative dissolves: "Faced with a threat to his entire future... he gives in."[9] After the humiliating failure to proceed as his conscience dictates, Alberto melts back into the comfortable oblivion of group membership. A few weeks after Richi's death, he is reintegrated into the same Miraflores patota that he left when he joined the perros at the Leoncio Prado academy. Richi's face becomes just another blurred image in a fading past: "Ahora podía recordar muchas cosas como si tratara de episodios de película. Pasaba días enteros sin encontrar el rostro del Esclavo" (328).

Other Vargasllosan protagonists are depicted as Conformers in more highly organized social institutions, such as the military. Lieutenant Gamboa in La ciudad , for example, is considered by officers and cadets as "el oficial modelo" (154). He differs markedly from his fellow officers: "Él amaba la vida militar precisamente por lo que otros la odiaban: La disciplina, la jeraquía, las campañas" (154). Gamboa perceives the military as a logically structured organization where justice prevails through order, and expresses complete faith in the system: "Un militar no arruina su carrera cumpliendo con su deber" (263). When Gamboa discovers that Richi's death was not accidental, he confidently follows group procedure, and demands a formal investigation of the incident. Gamboa's reward for loyalty is exile.

Captain Pantaleón Pantoja, protagonist of Pantaleón y las visitadoras, is a humorous counterpart of Gamboa. Like the Lieutenant in La ciudad, Pantoja surrenders himself completely to military regimentation: "Toda mi vida está en el Ejército" (308). He too feels that he must follow regulations to the limit: "Soy militar, tengo que cumplir con las órdenes" (213). His efficient organization of the Servicio de Visitadoras, and his public recognition of the slain Brasileña as "un valeroso soldado... una desdichada mártir del cumplimento del deber"(253), are comic examples of his unswerving devotion to the military. Ironically, Pantaleón, like Gamboa, is condemned by his group for his very devotion to its stated principles. Even though at the end of the novel Pantaleón believes that he has acted properly, "hice un buen trabajo" (298), he reacts differently to his sanction than does Gamboa. Like Alberto Fernández, he is ultimately too well incorporated into the group structure to protest his own castigation: "Reconozco mi responsabilidad. Aceptaré la sanción que se me dé por esa falta" (305).

Several patterns emerge in the analysis of this trio of Vargasllosan Conformers. Gamboa and Pantaleón are characters who become victimized by the group to which they are devoted. Punishment for loyalty leads to alienation and disillusion for Gamboa. Pantaleón Pantoja, while not regretting his actions, willingly accepts his punishment. Like Alberto in La ciudad , Pantaleón suppresses his individuality in deference to group standards.

A figure closely aligned with Pantaleón and Alberto is the narrator-protagonist of La tía Julia, Mario Vargas. Superficially, he appears to be a rebel rather than a Conformer. Close analysis shows that he is more concerned with conformity than with rebellion. The all-pervasive pandilla in Mario's life is his extended Limeñan family group. Nearly everyone that he comes in contact with is either a blood relative or an inlaw. He lives with his grandparents and socializes with his aunts and uncles. His best friend, Javier, is courting his cousin Nancy. The familial web of relations extends to the archbishop of Lima, who, as the narrator affirms, "era, por supuesto, pariente nuestro" (429-30). This ubiquitous family presence is recognized by Mario, who refers to it as a "clan" (241), and a "tribu familiar" (60).

Within this hierarchy, Mario, because of his youth, has a very low status. Throughout the narrative, he is constantly called upon to prove his maturity. His cousin Nancy, his friend Javier, and tía Julia taunt him with references to his age: "Pero si eres un bebe"(316); "... eres un mocoso (323); "Todavía eres un mocosito" (327). The young writer's nickname, the diminutive Marito, which is applied to him by his family, reinforces his inferior status in the group. He asserts that "Nada me irritaba tanto como el Marito; tenía la sensación de que el diminutivo me regresaba al pantalón corto" (16).

Considered in this light, Vargas' romance and elopement with tía Julia can be construed not as a rebellion from family values, but as an attempt to gain higher status within the clan. This motive is nowhere more evident than in the dialogue between Julia and Mario as the young student proposes to the middle-aged divorcée:

-¿Quieres casarte conmigo?--le pregunté. Se río con poca alegría. -Te estoy hablando en serio--insistí. -¿Me estás pidiendo que me case contigo de veras? - volvió a reírse la tía Julia, ahora sí más divertida. -¿Es sí o no - le dije ... -¿Me pides para demostrarle a tu familia que ya eres grande?-... También por eso - reconocí. (292-93)

Mario's marriage achieves its aim. After grave reservations, his father recognizes that "después de todo era un acto de hombría" (427). His "rebellion," therefore, is actually an atttempt to gain status and recognition in his family group. Mario, for all his bravado, is, like Alberto in La ciudad , ultimately revealed as a Conformer.

The image of a societal Victim is reflected to some extent in almost all of Vargas Llosa's characters. Several of his protagonists, however, possess characteristics that identify them almost exclusively with this image. Such characters often lack the necessary brute force or cunning to impose themelves upon society as Outsider figures often do. They are likewise unable to integrate themelves within groups or institutions for an extended period, as do the bulk of Vargasllosan Conformers. Neither predators nor participants, they become society's prey.

The particular circumstances of several Victims or scapegoats, such as Richi Arana in La ciudad and Pichula Cuéllar in Los cachorros, have been well-documented in critical studies of Vargas Llosa's narrative.[10] The female Victim is a recurring Vargasllosan character that finds its clearest manifestation in Bonifacia/La Selvática in Casa Verde, who is victimized repeatedly by successive groups and institutions. Kidnapped by nuns, who use her as a slave, she is expelled from their mission for an act of kindness interpreted as an act of rebellion. Raped by Lituma and left penniless and pregnant in Piura, she comes under Josefino's control, becomes a prostitute, and ultimately supports the incorrigible Inconquistables by selling her body.

Others who fit the same mold are Amalia and Hortensia in Conversación. The maid Amalia is victimized by her associates. She is drugged by her employer's son, who hopes to rape her while she is under the influence of the administered aphrodisiac. The young servant is fired for this incident, and this triggers a chain of events that inexorably leads to her death during childbirth in Pucallpa. Hortensia, Amalia's mistress at Cayo Bermúdez' residence, is abandoned by Bermúdez after the fall of the Odría government. Unable to fend for herself or to return to the position she held in society prior to her affair with Cayo, she sinks rapidly into a life of prostitution and drug addiction, a life which is brutally terminated by the ex-chauffeur Ambrosio in a back room of a cheap hotel. Jurema, in La guerra, is raped by the revolutionary Gall, hunted by her vengeance-seeking husband Rufino, nearly raped by Federal troops, and drawn against her will to the destruction in Canudos.

Victims, as these examples demonstrate, have no positive future in the Vargasllosan universe. As figures who are unwilling or unable to satisfy the whims of the social code, their existences are usually in decline from the outset of the novels they appear in. They are often absent at the novel's' conclusion.

The Outsider, the Conformer, and the Victim frequently come in contact with another ubiquitous Vargasllosan character, the Manipulator. This figure is generally a secondary character who is associated with a highly organized social institution; such as the military or a political party. Like the Conformer, the Manipulator is assimilated into group structure, but at a higher eschelon. He exercises considerable power and enjoys high status. Loyalty to group ideals, however, has no place in his value system. His highest priorities are self-preservation and self-aggrandizement.

The senior officers of the Leoncio Prado academy are prototypical Manipulators. The academy colonel, for example, knows that Richi Arana's death wound is not self-inflicted. Nevertheless, to avoid complications, he withholds the truth: "Lo más sensato es mantener la tesis de un error cometido por el propio cadete. Hay que cortar de raíz cualquier rumor, cualquier comentario" (215). The colonel and his subordinates are prepared "to cover up even a murder to protect their jobs and their illusions."[11]

This type of self-centered expediency is paralleled in other military figures in _Pantaleón_. General Felipe Collazos and his cronies, General Victoria and Colonel López López, initiate the Servicio de Visitadoras and place Captain Pantoja in charge of its operation. When the novice cafiche's military status becomes known, the shock waves reach the office of the Minister of War. Collazos, however, accepts no responsibility for the plan that he and his fellow officers developed. He deftly transfers the blame for the visitadora service to Pantaleón. At the novel's end, Pantoja is exiled to an isolated post in the Peruvian puna, while Collazos, Victoria, and López López remain comfortably ensconced in their Lima offices.

The Manipulator resurfaces in Casa Verde in the figure of Julio Reátegui. He uses his political façade of provincial governor to control economic and commercial activity in the Amazon region. When local Indians attempt to establish a cooperative to sell their rubber, Reátegui reacts predictably. In order to maintain his illegal monopoly, he orders the arrest and torture of Jum, the principal Indian instigator. In this manner, Reátegui's civil authority becomes a front for the pursuit and maintenance of personal profit.

Vargas Llosa's skill in highlighting the characteristics of the Manipulator is reflected in the person of Germán Laúdano Rosales, el Sinchi in Pantaleón. Rosales is the "untuoso e hipócrita periodista radial,"[12] whose broadcasts punctuate the narrative. His popularity enables him to influence public opinion

71

in the jungle community of Iquitos. When Rosales' blackmail requests go unheeded by Pantaleón, he launches an impassioned campaign against the evils of the prostitute service and its founder. After the broadcaster begins to receive a monthly sum of five hundred soles from Captain Pantoja, his moral position changes dramatically: "-El Supremo Gobierno debería condecorar con la Orden de Sol al señor Pantaleón Pantoja -- estalla...dramatiza y exige La Voz del Sinchi.- Por la encomiástica labor que realiza en procura de la satisfacción de la necesidades íntimas de los centinelas del Perú"(234-35).

Like other Manipulators, el Sinchi's true concern with society extends no further than the limits of expediency and self-interest.

In La guerra, the Manipulator resurfaces as a political figure, Epamonidas Gonçalves. The opportunistic Gonçalves, a Republican Party leader, secretly hires the anarchist Galileo Gall to transport arms to Canudos. He then denounces Gall as an English agent hired by Brazilian royalists to destroy the Republic. His propagandistic duplicity succeeds, and wins him political control of the state of Bahia. In a conciliatory speech directed to Epamonidas Gonçalves, his former adversary, the Barón de Cañabrava, summarizes the qualities of this version of Vargas Llosa's Manipulator: "Hemos entrado en la hora de la acción, de la audacia, de la violencia, incluso de los crímenes. Ahora se trata

72

de disociar totalmente la política de la moral. Estando así las cosas, la persona mejor preparada para mantener el orden en este estado es usted"(331).

The concept of characterological modes in textual analysis assists in the postulation of larger assumptions with respect to Vargas Llosa's novelistic production. If, as René Wellek and Austin Warren assert, it is customary to speak of all narrative plots as involving conflicts between "man against nature, or man against other men, or man fighting with himself,"[13] Vargas Llosa's plots, judging from the data gleaned from his examination, fall almost exclusively into the "man against man" category. Within this range, individuals of protagonistic importance are either Outsiders fighting against society, Conformers whose quarrel is with a particular group, or random Victims of society's rage or indifference. In any case, a main character has an extremely limited possibility of success against such unscrupulous secondary figures as the Manipulator. Within the framework of Northrup Frye's generic systems established in his Anatomy of Criticism.[14] Vargas Llosa's protagonists, whose power for interaction with others is extremely limited, become clear representatives of the ironic mode of fiction.

Characters of protagonistic importance in Vargas Llosa's narrative frequently are presented in three separate modalities. Each mode is determined by the nature and extent of the individual's social interactions with groups. The patterns of Outsider, Conformer, and Victim that surface in the Peruvian writer's novels represent a spectrum that extends from a nucleus of group harmony to the extremes of acceptance and rejection. The persistent, limited range of individual potential that is reflected in such modalities extends their significance beyond the individual works in which they appear into an ironic general comment on the nature of human relationships.

NOTES

[1]Bernard Berelson and Gary A. Steiner, Human Behavior (New York: Harcourt, Brace and World, 1964) 328.

[2]Christopher Gillie, Character in English Fiction (New York: Barnes and Noble, 1965) 156.

[3]José Luis Martín, La narrativa de Vargas Llosa (Madrid: Editorial Gredos, 1974) 106.

[4] Rosa Boldori de Baldussi, Vargas Llosa: un narrador y sus demonios (Buenos Aires: Fernando García Cambeiro, 1974) 94.

[5] Casto M. Fernández, Aproximación formal a la novelística de Vargas Llosa (Madrid: Editorial Nacional, 1977) 104.

[6]Malcom Bradbury, "An Approach Through Structure," in Towards a Poetics of Fiction, ed. Mark Spilka (Bloomington: Indiana UP, 1977): 10.

[7]Luis A. Díez, Vargas Llosa's Pursuit of the Total Novel (Cuernavaca: Centro Intercultural de Documentación, 1970), C. 1, 52.

[8]Díez 53.

[9]Díez 54.

[10]See for example, Mary A. Davis' "Mario Vargas Llosa: The Necessary Scapegoat," Texas Studies in Literature and Language, 19 (1977): 540-43, and the aforementioned José Luis Martín's La narrativa de Vargas Llosa, Chapter 3.

[11]"No Fomentor," London Times Literary Supplement, 9 Jan. 1964: 21.

[12]José Miguel Oviedo, Mario Vargas Llosa: la invención de una realidad 2nd ed. (Barcelona: Barral Editores, 1977) 275.

[13]René Wellek and Austin Warren, Theory of Literature (New York: Harcourt, Brace and World, 1956) 217.

---

[14]See Frye's <u>Anatomy of Criticism</u>, 3rd ed. (Princeton: Princeton Univ. Press, 1973) 33-67.

Chapter 5

Rites of Passage

Mario Vargas Llosa has described the craft of fiction as a species of exorcism in which writers achieve catharsis by transforming their personal demons into the themes of their literary works.[1] Although extensive critical acknowledgement of the recurring depiction of the problems of adolescent Peruvian males in La ciudad y los perros and Los cachorros supports the contention that this reiterated thematic concern is one of the author's own "demonios personales," Vargas Llosa's literary preoccupation with adolescent rites of passage in fact encompasses a period of more than twenty years in his writing, commencing in his earliest fiction, and recurring sporadically through his fifth novel, the autobiographical La tía Julia y el escribidor.

Vargas Llosa's chronicle of adolescent passages has two phases. The first deals with what psychologist Erik Erikson terms "elemental" problems of early and mid-adolescence: the development of a sense of identity and the process of social adjustment.[2] These notions surface primarily in earlier works

76

such as Los jefes , La ciudad, and Los cachorros. A second phase, which has been less-frequently recognized by most critics to date, places greater emphasis on problems often associated with late adolescence: the search for a vocation, the development of a world view, and concern with the process of becoming an adult. These preoccupations appear in Conversación en la catedral and in La tía Julia y el escribidor. A review of the recurrence of the adolescent theme in all these works confirms Vargas Llosa's compulsion to depict the way of life between childhood and adulthood. Moreover, it can be observed that the author's treatment of the subject undergoes a subtle evolution that itself parallels the stages in an individual's metamorphosis from child to adult.

Two of the six stories in Vargas Llosa's first book, Los jefes deal with adolescent passages. The title piece, written about 1953, is, by the author's admission, his earliest extant work of fiction.[3] Its plot recounts the attempt of a band of colegio students to organize a protest strike over exam scheduling at their school. The instigators, including the anonymous narrator, are a small, close-knit band of adolescent males, the Coyotes. While their hostility ostensibly is directed toward adult authority figures, the true conflict is a struggle for supremacy between two individuals, the youthful narrator, a deposed leader of the group, and the Oriental interloper, Lu. The student strike fails due to lack of group solidarity, and the story ends with the establishment of an uneasy truce between the two protagonists.

Like "Los jefes", Día domingo", another story in the collection, begins on one thematic note and ends on a different one. Miguel, a member of the Pajarracos, a group similar in philosophy and composition to the Coyotes declares his love to Flora, a pubescent colegio student. The reader soon learns that Miguel's romantic interest stems at least in part from a personal vendetta with Rubén, a youth who has replaced him as leader of the Pajarracos, and who also courts Flora. In order to prevent a prearranged meeting between Rubén and Flora, Miguel challenges his rival to a dangerous swimming match that nearly costs the pair their lives. At story's end, Miguel temporarily wins the right to court Flora, but his status in the group and his relationship with Rubén remains uncertain.

The parallels in the stories are noteworthy, for both protagonists' primary concern is not what is appears to be. Both actually seek to establish or maintain an identity and a status in their respective pandillas. The disparity between their stated goals of student solidarity and romantic involvement and the individuals' true needs creates an irony that contributes to the story's effectiveness while demonstrating Vargas Llosa's primordial interest in depicting the crises in adolescent development.

The young male's quest for identity and search for social acceptance becomes the primary focus of a more extensive inquiry in the author's next work, La ciudad. Here the monologues and dialogues of Richi, Alberto, Jaguar, and Boa offer different perspectives on the subject of adolescent adaptation. The Leoncio Prado Military Academy brings together teen-age males of differing economic status but with similar adjustment problems. Avenues for emotional and psychological growth are limited or non-existent in the oppressive Academy atmosphere. Each cadet arrives with his own emotional baggage, a burden that helps to explain the choice of a method of coping with the rites of passage in the new peer group.

Richi Arana's relationship with a submissive mother and a distant, domineering father denies him the emotional stability to deal with his new colleagues. Naturally subservient, "el Esclavo" can identify with no one in his new environment. His social "death" foretells his physical death. Alberto Fernández, like Richi, comes from an upper-middle class background, and has a submissive mother and frequently-absent father. Unlike his counterpart, however, Alberto had developed some sense of identity and some ability for social interaction within his neighborhood peer group. At the Leoncio Prado he conforms and dissimulates, an approach that wins him acceptance among the perros, but which brings with it no satisfactory interpersonal relationships.

The familial histories of two lower-class protagonists, Boa and Jaguar are likewise similar. Both youths are fatherless and have indifferent mothers. Their respective male role-models are a brutish older brother and thief. Identifications with these two figures helps to explain their approach to developing relationships with peers at the Academy. Boa imposes his will by brute force, engendering a fear that precludes the development of friendships. This fact is highlighted in his monologues, which are directed to his only companion, the dog la Malpapeada. The enigmatic Jaguar, reminiscent of Lu in the story "Los jefes", attains a leadership position through a combination of strength and cunning, but he instills no loyalty and develops no friendships.

The adolescent themes in the early stories of Vargas Llosa stress the individual's struggle to achieve a position of leadership and identity in the peer group. In La ciudad the dominance of certain individuals is an established fact from the novel's outset. Hence, the emphasis on the possible modes of accommodation within the group's infrastructure. If the stories conclusion is stalemate, the novel's becomes a veritable dead end in three cases, and in a fourth case, that of Richi, a literal dead end.

A final analysis of this phase in adolescent development is presented in Los cachorros, published five years after La ciudad. In this novella Cuéllar, the putative protagonist, initially is a popular member of his group, the Cachorros. Nevertheless, his accidental castration ultimately precludes his acceptance in the pandilla when his friends reach puberty and seek positive relationships with the opposite sex. In the case of Cuéllar, as in the case of Richi/el Esclavo in La ciudad, the imposition of a depreciatory nickname, Pichula, verbally marks him as an adolescent misfit and outcast. A unique component of the novella is the unusual perspective from which the story is presented. Most of the action is relayed by an ubiquitous narrator that reflects the collective point of view of the Cachorros. This frightening perspective of anonymity and strict adherence to a social code helps to paint a vivid portrait of the extremes of adolescent peer-group conformity.

Los cachorros brings to a close the first phase of Vargas Llosa's literary depictions of the crises of adolescence. In this stage he analyzed the notions of identity and social acceptance from the perspective of strong and weak youths, the wealthy and the poor, the emotionally stable and the psychologically deprived, as well as from the point of view of the peer group itself. His conclusions are disturbingly similar. Almost all of the adolescent males dealt with are socially isolated individuals with an unclear sense of self who follow ritualized patterns of behavior and communication, and who seemingly are uncapable of establishing meaningful interpersonal relationships.

Although unable to arrive at any positive solutions to the adolescent problems described in his early works, Vargas Llosa has continued to seek answers in his fiction. Two later novels, Conversación and La tía Julia. reveal a different approach to the theme.

Among the many concerns dealt with in Conversación are the difficulties that the protagonist Santiago Zavala encounters during the life-phrase that Daniel J. Levinson, in The Seasons of a Man's Life defines as the "novice phase of early adult transition" (from age 18-22).[4] The eight-year time span of the novel takes Zavala from the age of eighteen to age twenty-six, and thus includes this developmental stage. A member of a wealthy Limeñan family, the protagonist apparently avoided or postponed those necessary changes in early adolescence that his precursors faced prior in Vargas Llosan fiction. His tasks in this later period, such as locating himself in a peer group and finding a comfortable sex role, ideology, and occupation are thus all the more formidable. Santiago's approach to coping with these critical processes is conspicuously extreme. He attends a non-fashionable university, seeks a low-status job as a newspaper reporter, socializes with political revolutionaries, and marries a chola. It is noteworthy that these decisions correspond exactly to those described by Levinson in The Seasons of a Man's Life as typical of the period; namely, a change in ethnic attachments and lifestyle, change in religious affiliation or identity, marriage to a woman of a different social background, and movement into a class or subculture very different in values and outlook from that of the parents. In Zavalita's case, such actions are in essence merely reactions to the status-quo of his late-adolescent world. Predictably, they do not in themselves contribute to personal growth and development, but only lead to cynicism and a general sense of malaise. Carlitos, Zavalita's newspaper colleague, recognizes his friend's stagnation and communicates this knowledge to Zavala during his conversation: "Pareces una puta vieja que recuerda su juventud, Zavalita ... parece que hubieras dejado de vivir cuando tenías dieciocho años" (172). Stalled in the transition stage between adolescence and adulthood, Zavala is reduced to endless and unproductive self-injury: "se había jodido en algún momento. Piensa: ¿en cuál?" (13).

Unlike Zavalita, who rejects his family origins in the novice adult phase, Mario Vargas, the protagonist of La tía Julia, devotes his energies to seeking reintegration in his familial group as an adult. Almost all of his relationships are with blood relatives or in-laws. He lives with his grandparents, and socializes with his aunts and uncles. Within the family, Mario has a very low status because of his age. Throughout the narrative, he constantly is called upon to prove his maturity and is frequently taunted by his relatives who make references to his youth: "Pero sí eres un bebe" (326); "eres un mocoso, no tienes una profesión ni donde caerte muerto" (405); "todavía eres un mocosito" (327). His familial nickname, the diminutive of Marito, reinforces his inferior status: "nada me irritaba tanto como el Marito, tenía, la sensación de que el diminutivo me regresaba al pantalón corto" (16). In order to convince the family of his maturity, Mario performs what he considers a mature act by marrying Julia, a distant relative almost twice his age. He admits his ulterior motive to Julia when she questions him about his proposal: "¿Me pides para demonstrarle a tu familia que ya eres grande?...--También por eso-reconocí" (292). Mario's impulsive marriage achieves its immediate aim. After grave reservations, his father recognizes that, "después de todo, era un acto de hombría" (427). Julia likewise confirms her husband's new-found maturity: "Vaya Varguitas ... te estás haciendo un hombrecito" (428). From the standpoint of actual personal development, however, the elopement represents a regression rather than a progression. Gail Sheehy, noting the danger of such a decision in her book, Passages, summarizes the actual consequences of Mario's hasty marriage.[5] Sheehy asserts that we can piggyback our development by attaching to a "Stronger One," but those who marry during this time period often prolong financial and emotional ties to family and relatives that impede them from becoming self-sufficient. Predictably, Mario's marriage ends in divorce. Unpredictably, and ironically, he apparently compounds this error of judgement later in the novice adult period by marrying for a second time to a yet-closer relative, his first cousin, Patricia.

In this final stage in the depiction of adolescent passages, Vargas Llosa presents two radical and diametrically opposed approaches to the development crises of the period. Zavala in Conversación seeks a total and immediate termination of the relationships with family and the pre-adult aspects of the self. Mario, in contrast, manifests a strong need to perpetuate his dependency on the family and remain fixed in an immature child-mother relationship. Both approaches substitute extreme reactions for positive actions, and are thus programmed to end in failure.

During a period of over thirty years of literary activity, Mario Vargas Llosa has persistently sought to exorcise the demons of his youth by portraying adolescent crises in his fiction. In the course of this endeavor, he has examined systematically almost every phase in the transition from child to adult in detail, often alluding to his own intimate and personal life-experiences in the process. The success of Vargas Llosa's male protagonists

85

in coping with the problem of adolescence is minimal, and their personal failure is an implicit indictment of a society, which, by virtue of its Hispanic heritage, places great emphasis on the development of interpersonal relations through a network of small, intimate infrastructures -- precisely those infrastructures described by the author. In the course of this project, Vargas Llosa has given us some of the most enduring and powerful works of contemporary Latin American fiction. One hopes coincidentally that the process has resulted in a therapeutic personal catharsis for the author.

NOTES

[1] Mario Vargas Llosa, Gabriel García Márquez: historia de un deicidio (Barcelona: Monte Avila Editores, 1971) 87.

[2] see "The Eight Stages of Man," in Erik Erikson, Childhood and Society (New York: Norton Press, 1950) 219-233.

[3] "Author's Preface," In Mario Vargas Llosa, The Cubs and Other Stories (New York: Norton Press, 1950) 219-233.

[4] Daniel J. Levinson, The Seasons of a Man's Life (New York: Knopt, 1978) 71-78.

[5] Gail Sheehy, Passages: Predictable Crises of Adult Life (New York: Bantam Books, 1977) 94-97.

Chapter Six

Dreams and Dreamers

Pantaleón y las visitadoras is the only novel by Mario
Vargas Llosa that employs actual dream sequences of sleeping
characters as a narrative strategy.[1] While the presence of
dreams in the novel is duly noted by the critics,[2] their function
and significance have not been explored adequately. Vargas Llosa,
commenting on this critical lacuna, has asserted that the dream
segments in Pantaleón y las visitadoras remain "the least
understood parts of the novel."[3] This essay sugests that the
dream sequences are carefully devised narrative components that
contribute significantly to plot and character development while
reinforcing thematic concerns in the work.

The novel relates the story of Pantaleón Pantoja, a Peruvian
military officer who is ordered to create a secret,
governmentally-sanctioned prostitution service, the SVGPFA
(Servicio de Visitadoras para Guarniciones, Puestos de Frontera y
Afines), in his country's Amazon outposts. A blend of dialogue,
military memoranda, letters, radio emissions, and newspaper
texts documents the founding, flourishing, and demise of

Pantoja's service. Three dreams that the protagonist experiences also are woven into the fabric of the narrative.

The first dream, in which Pantaleón reviews troops for a parade, occurs shortly after he arrives in Iquitos to begin his new assignment. Initially, a series of innocuous memories of his prior military post in Chiclayo merge to create an aura of well-being for the dreamer. The dream transforms into a humiliating nightmare in its second stage as Pantoja's male soldiers metamorphose into seductive, scantily-clad females in front of his superiors. In the dream's third phase, four figures in the retinue become individually distinguishable. The first three are recognized as Iquitan residents associated with local bordellos. As the nightmare ends, the horrified Pantoja notes that the fourth figure is his weeping wife, Pochita.

The first dream sequence establishes a pattern of form and content that is duplicated in the remaining dreams of the novel, where both the tripartite division and the motif of metamorphosis are repeated. The dream's contribution to plot development is subtle yet significant. In the nightmare, which takes place on August 16, 1956, civilians metamorphose into military personnel. Leonor Curinchila, a madam, wears a uniform, and her assistant, Chupito, is dressed as a quarter-master. The pimp Porfirio Wong appears as a second-lieutenant. Nevertheless, Pantaleón, in later correspondence with his superiors, notes that these three characters were not hired as military assistants until three days after his dream. The first oneiric sequence thus anticipates later plot developments in the novel.

From the standpoint of character, the dream sequences of Pantaleón collectively offer "the only psychological pentration of Pantoja in the novel."[4] Significantly, the first nightmare does not reinforce known traits of the protagonist, but rather reveals a wide range of attitudes that contrast with those exhibited in his stoic public façade. The dreamer's emotions here progress from "nostalgia" and "tristeza" to "miedo" and "terror frío" (54), and from "humillación" and "vergüenza" (56) to "angustia" (58). An important contributing factor to Pantoja's oneiric distress is his concern that his wife and mother will discover the true nature of his assignment. Negative feelings temporarily are replaced by an accompanying incipiently erotic element: "Una sensación de placer ávido, de satisfacción animal, de alegría exasperada y tentacular, borran el miedo, la nostalgia, el ridículo, mientras las reclutas pellizcan, acarician y mordisquean las orejas del teniente Pantoja" (57).

The contrast between such strong emotions and sensations, and the reserved, subservient waking behavior of Pantaleón is heightened by the positioning of the first dream segment in the text between two impersonal military reports sent by the protagonist to his superior, General Collazos. Pantoja's

89

impressions during the dream state contradict those dutifully recorded in the communiqués. In the first report, for example, Pantoja praises his new commander, General Scavino, for his "amabilidad y cordial simpatía" (37). In his dream, however, he reveals a different perception of Scavino: "El trago no sería tan amargo si no estuvieran también allí...amonestándolo con tristeza, furia y decepción, los ojos grises del general Scavino" (56-57). The patriotic enthusiasm with which Pantoja details the initial phases of his assignment in his letters likewise contrasts with feelings about the project that subsequently surface in his dream: "Nadie sabe que maldice su suerte. Su dolor es profundo, grande su humillación, infinita su vergüenza ...." (56).

Pantoja's second nightmare occurs two weeks after his first. It commences with three flashbacks that chronicle his long struggle with an embarrassing and painful medical ailment, hemorrhoids. In the second phase this humiliating problem is linked with his present emotional stress. The operation that relieved his pain is re-enacted, while familiar figures, who were not present at the time, metamorphose in front of the dreamer. General Collazos, Pantaleón's superior, becomes the pimp Wong; Pantaleón's mother assumes the physical characteristics of the Iquitan madam, Leonor Curinchila. The dwarf Chupito transforms into a monkey after introducing the first two visitadora recruits. A second military officer, General Victoria, notes the addition of two more visitadoras to the service. Phase three of the dream details Pantaleón's post-operative pain, which is partially induced by a prescribed enema. As the nightmare ends, he awaits the effects of the procedure, repeatedly asserting, "no cagaré visitadoras" (84).

The scatological second dream repeats the three-part structure and metamorphosis motif of the first nightmare. Additionally, Pantoja's fear that his mother or his wife may discover the nature of his assignment resurfaces, providing another thematic link with the earlier dream segment. Several elements in the second dream illustrate the worsening of the protagonist's psychological state. The erotic cosquilleo caused by the anonymous visitadoras' caresses in the first dream contrasts here with the memory of the consquilleo atormentador that Pantoja associates with his hemorrhoids. Character transmutations become more radical, and include the appearance of doubles. These figures echo the growing duplicity of Pantaleón's existence as he shuttles between his normal home life and his secret role of military pimp. Occurring at the end of Chapter Three of the novel, the scatological nightmare offers a striking contrast to the first half of the chapter, in which Pochita Pantoja, in a frivolous letter to her sister, displays an ignorance of the nature of his new assignment. Finally, the mention of the hiring of the first four visitadoras in the dream

91

represents the only notification of such recruitment in the narrative. Information in Pantoja's first dream served to prefigure plot; in the second dream, recruiting details further plot development.

Eighteen months intervene between the novel's first oneiric sequences and the final dream segment. In the interim, the state of Pantaleón's private life deteriorates in inverse proportion to the success of the SVGPFA. Although the number of prostitutes and support personnel increases dramatically, the non-military community, abetted by the diatribes of the radio personality, el Sinchi, condemns the endeavor. Pochita Pantoja gives birth to the couple's first child, but abandons Pantaleón upon learning the nature of his military duties and of his affair with the prostitute, la Brasileña. At the apex of his career and at the nadir of his personal life, Pantoja experiences a final nightmare.

As the dream begins, Pantoja muses on the loss of his child and wife, and anticipates a recurrence of the terrifying doubles and metamorphoses. Pantaleón is reassured temporarily when five normal soldiers appear, leading five dogs in parade: "He perdido a mi esposa y a mi hija, pero, al menos, lo que va a ocurrir aquí no será tan atroz como otras veces" (207). The dogs, however, soon transform into ape-like monsters, and the monsters then metamorphose into familiar, dual-identify characters. Pantoja's mother, Señora Leonor, and the madam Leonor

92

Curinchila again coalesce. General Collazos blends with el Sinchi. The dwarf Chupito shares characteristics with General Scavino, and the pimp Wong now bears a resemblance to the Chaplain, Padre Beltrán. The fifth figure is Pochita Pantoja, who wore a visitadora recruit uniform in Pantoja's first dream. She now has transformed completely into la Brasileña, her husband's mistress.

The three-phase metamorphosis (perros-monstruos-dobles) witnessed here by Pantaleón reiterates and synthesizes the pattern established in the earlier dreams. Both the desfile of the first dream and the dobles of the second are combined by the dreamer in the third dream: "El maldito desfile de los dobles otra vez" (206). Other contrasting elements reinforce the concept of the now total dominance of the visitadora service lifestyle in Pantaleón's waking existence. For example, while the earlier dreams began with past recollections, the final dream is presented exclusively in the present, and takes place entirely at the SVGPFA's centro logístico. The partial metamorphosis and doubling of dream characters evident in the initial dreams is now complete, and is reinforced by the onomastic duplicity employed by Pantoja in identifying individuals. Sinchi Collazos, for example blends the nickname of the radio personality Germán Laúdano Rosales and the last name of Pantoja's superior officer. Similar amalgams employed in the third dream are Chupito Scavino and el padre Porfirio. The definitive oneiric

93

metamorphosis graphically demonstrates Pantaleón's anguish over the fact that all figures formerly associated with authority and decorum (mother, commanding officers, chaplain, wife) have been transformed into pimps, opportunists, madams, and prostitutes.

The third nightmare segment is placed strategically in the text at the peak of the visitadora service's influence and popularity. It precedes by one chapter the account of la Brasileña's death, the unforeseen event that hastens the demise of the SVGPFA. Its dream-montage effectively summarizes plot development, reviews the roles and influence of the major characters in the work, and demonstrates the telling psychological effect of these people and events on the protagonist.

Besides contributing to plot and character, the dream clusters have a symbolic value. Collectively they reflect thematic concerns in the novel. Pantoja's dreams are induced by his forced waking participation in an endeavor that is dream-like in its ludicrousness. The potentially tragic personal ramifications of the visitadora service envisioned by Pantoja are no more absurd than the ultimate consequences of the project. His greatest fear is that his relatives may learn of the nature of his assignment. His superiors show a similar concern with keeping secret the military's role in the affair. The dreams

94

feature dobles who epitomize the subversion of traditional values and authority, a subversion that finds a parallel in the enforced confidentiality, camouflage, and duplicity employed by the army to maintain the SVGPFA.

The link between Pantaleón, the nightmares, and reality is forged definitively in the novel's last chapter, which functions as an epilogue. Here, Pantoja's superiors and associates refer to his waking activities in oneiric terms. General Collazos, a metamorphosing monster in the dreams, calls the defunct SVGPFA a "monstruosidad que se le antojó hacer allá en Iquitos" (305). Pantaleón's military contact and confidante, Lieutenant Bacacorzo, fears that his friend's "delirium" may be contagious: "No sé qué me pasó, me contagiaría usted su delirio" (280). General Scavino also notes the strange effect of Pantoja's influence: "Tengo la sensación de estar soñando, Pantoja. Me hace usted sentir que todo es irreal, una pesadilla..." (287). Ultimately Scavino links the SVGPFA to another societal nightmare, the ill-fated religious cult of Hermano Francisco: "en fin, las dos pesadillas de la Amazonia terminaron una vez por todas" (305). The visitadora service creates a societal pesadilla that is reflected on an individual level in the metamorphic nightmares of its founder.

Pantaleón Pantoja's three dreams, interspersed strategically in the text, successfully and successively prefigure, advance and summarize plot development. Collectively they provide a surrealistic résumé of the rise and fall of the visitadora service while painting a portrait of the protagonist that is more complex and more human than his public image suggests. Ultimately, the notions of the dreamer, the nightmare, duplicity, and the subversion of the social order that appear in the dreams are reinforced and reiterated on a broader social level in the "waking" portions of Vargas Llosa's novel.

NOTES

[1]Vargas Llosa employs a related strategy, the use of dream-like reveries, in an earlier novel, La ciudad y los perros (1962). See Chapter Two of this study for an analysis of this technique.

[2]Rosa Boldori de Baldussi's brief discussion of the dream segments in her study, Vargas Llosa: un narrador y sus demonios (Buenos Aires: Fernando García Cambeiro, 1974): 134-36, represents the only prior attempt to analyze systematically the oneiric sequences. She concludes that the dreams help to reveal "facetas complementarias de la psicología del personaje," and provide "la apertura a nuevas dimensions temporales."

[3]Mario Vargas Llosa, "The Genesis and Evolution of Pantaleón y las visitadoras," trans. Raquel Chang-Rodríguez and Gabriela de Beer, The City College Papers, 12 (March, 1977) 13.

[4]Raymond L. Williams, "The Narrative Art of Mario Vargas Llosa: Two Organizing Principles in Pantaleón y las visitadoras," Texas Studies in Literature and Language 19 (1977: 78.

Chapter Seven

Choral Characters

Although traditionally associated with classic Greek drama, the chorus was adopted successfully for use in narrative by many nineteenth and early twentieth-century novelists. Both Thomas Hardy and Sir Walter Scott employed choruses of rustic characters in their novels. The group of good wives in the first scenes of Hawthorne's The Scarlet Letter, and the confidantes or ficelles of Henry James' fiction are further examples of the successful borrowing of this dramatic device for use in fiction. Choral characters in narrative resurface in a revitalized form in the early novels of Mario Vargas Llosa, and they are skillfully employed to achieve diverse aims. In three works, Los cachorros, La Casa Verde, and Conversación en la Catedral, several figures serve collectively as a single character, forming a chorus or group protagonist. The function of the choral character differs in each work.

In Book Two of Conversación, twenty-eight sequences that detail the life of Cayo Bermúdez' mistress Hortensia at the political strongman's residence are presented from the perspective of the three household maids, Amalia, Símula, and

97

Carlota. Amalia later becomes a clearly individuated figure in the novel, while Carlota and Símula disappear. At this point in the work, however, the triad of servants provides information about important events in the story. The introduction of the characters of Hortensia and her lesbian lover, Queta, the Hortensia/Cayo Bermúdez/Queta sexual relationship, and the first news of don Cayo's fall from political power and flight to Brazil are all presented through the perspective of these "humildes medios de información."[1]

The group protagonist assumes an equally important role in an earlier novella, Los cachorros. In this work the putative main character, Cuéllar, is developed strictly from the external perspective of his adolescent peer group, los Cachorros, and never from any personal, internal vantage point. Cuéllar is, as José Miguel Oviedo notes, no more than "una especie de emanación de su pandilla, el indefenso objeto de sus miradas."[2] The opening paragraph of the work, with its shifting first and third person plural verb forms, sets a collective narrative pattern that is maintained throughout the story: "Todavía llevaban patalón corto ese año, aún no fumábamos, entre los deportes preferían el fútbol y estábamos aprendiendo a correr olas...y eran traviesos, lampiños, curiosos...Ese año, cuando Cuéllar entró al colegio..."(53). While the unusual device of shifting person is the stylistic hallmark of the group los Cachorros, this chorus is not simply the narrator, but also the true protagonist of the novel. Its narration does not cease upon Cuéllar's death, and its members, acting "strictly according to the rules and code of their class,"[3] continue to mature as proper bourgeoisie. Although Cuéllar is an interesting social misfit, the adolescent chorus, typified by its ruthless laws of conformity, ultimately assumes the main role in the novel as a group protagonist.

The choral role of a minor group, la Orquesta, in Vargas Llosa's third novel, La Casa Verde, is crucial to the development of what has been termed the "climax dramático del libro,"[4] a Russian roulette challenge between the Piuran resident Seminario and Sergeant Lituma. The Orquesta, which consists of the trio Bolas, el Joven, and el Arpista, had, up to this point in the novel, functioned chiefly as a colorful representative of barrio life in Piura.[5] The Russian roulette incident, which the chorus la Orquesta relates, is a watershed that divides the existences of two dual-personality protagonists, Bonifacia/la Selvática and Lituma/el Sargento. Because of the duel, el Sargento "volverá a su condición de Lituma y Bonifacia se convertirá en la Selvática."[6] Long after the event, Bonifacia, working at a brothel under the pseudonym la Selvática, asks el Arpista, one of the few witnesses to the duel, for details of the tragedy. The blind harpist can only relate to her the words that he heard that night. Bolas and el Joven, however, assist their musical partner in recounting the incident that they all witnessed by adding details and setting the scene for both la Selvática and the reader. In four sequences from Part Three of the novel, their collective choral voice systematically recounts the event that is of pivotal importance in the lives of Bonifacia and Lituma. Significantly, it is at this point in the narrative that the characters of Lituma and el Sargento merge, for the passage describing the climax of the event begins by referring to him by his name, and concludes by referring to him by his title:

> Lituma soltó el tambor, había que sortear para ver quién comenzaba, pero qué importa, él lo convidó así que alzó la pistola, le tocaba, puso la boca del caño en su sien, se cierra los ojos, y cerró los ojos, y se dispara y apretó el gatillo: tac y un castañeo de dientes. Se puso pálido ... El Sargento había colocado el revólver en la mesa y estaba bebiendo despacio .... (294, my emphasis)

While providing the narrative that links the character of Lituma with el Sargento, and the figure of Bonifacia with la Selvática, the figure of Bonifacia with la Selvática, the chorus la Orquesta also evokes the past recollections of another choral group, los Inconquistables. This trio of recalcitrants, consisting of Mono, José, and Josefino, furnishes extra information about Lituma and Bonifacia that colors the reader's perspective of the incident that ultimately is responsible for their separation. From los Inconquistables, for example, we learn the details of Lituma's return to his hometown with his bride Bonifacia. Additionally,

100

Josefino's designs on Bonifacia prior to her separation from her husband are outlined. In sum, the lives of two major protagonists in Casa Verde, Lituma and Bonifacia, are presented in this section of the novel almost exclusively through the reminiscences of two choruses, la Orquesta and los Inconquistables.

Although none of the individual figures that comprise any of these choral groups has the depth of a well-rounded character, collectively they often reveal the diversity and complexity common in a single protagonist. One example of this blending of characteristics occurs in Casa Verde, where the distinct viewpoints of el Joven, Bolas, and el Arpista coalesce to provide the reader with a vivid reenactment of the Seminario-Lituma duel. El Arpista concentrates on the verbal aspects of the event in his descriptions to la Selvática: "Sólo te puedo contar lo que se oyó esa noche, muchacha ... te habrás dado cuenta que casi no veo" (223). The dialogue between Lituma and Seminario that appears in the text is actually being recalled dramatically by the aged musician. Bolas, in contrast offers a wealth of objective visual details in his commentary on the duel that describe the setting, those present, and the witnesses' physical reactions to the incident:

-Sólo había dos clientes cuando entraron--dijo el Bolas--.
En la mesa ésa. Uno de ellos era Seminario (223);

-- ... él (Seminario) estaba de malas -- dijo el Bolas--. Se

101

Había picado por algo y buscaba pelea (225);

--Y entonces la Chunga vino corriendo y se les puso en medio.
¡Eras más valiente! --dijo el Bolas (273);

Y él (Lituma) nos tenía embrujados a nosotros--dijo el bolas--,
y Seminario le obedecía como su cholito. Apenas Lituma le
ordenó eso, abrió su revólver y le sacó todas las balas menos
una. Le temblaban los dedos al pobre.(293)

The words and gestures of the third member of the chorus, el
Joven, add an emotional note to Bolas' objective descriptions.
Replete with references to anger and rage, and accompanied by
the narrator's sighs and melancholic gestures, these details
dramatically enhance the aura of foreboding and fear that
dominates the scene:

--Así comienzan a veces las desgracias --dijo con gesto melancólico--. Por una
canción (224);

--Un toro de hombre ese Seminario --dijo el Joven--.Y una mirada maligna. Más
fuerte eres, más malo eres (225);

--Seminario llegaba aquí tranquilo, pero a las dos copas se enfurecía. Debía tener
alguna pena terrible en el corazón, y la desfogaba así con lisuras y trompadas (245);

--Como esos enamorados que uno les habla y les habla y es de balde porque andan en
la luna -- suspiró el Joven--. A Lituma lo tenía embrujado el cachorrito. (293)

The blending of the three musicians' distinct impressions of the
incident, el Arpista's verbal recollections, Bolas' vivid visual
summary, and el Joven's emotional addenda, thus provide sensory
and psychological impressions that combine to recreate in

accurate detail a scene of considerable importance to the action of the novel.

The function and nature of the choral triad of Amalia, Símula, and Carlota in Conversación is distinct from that of la Orquesta in Casa Verde. As they supply information about the Hortensia--Queta - don Cayo sexual relationship, their collective naiveté provides a humble working-class background against which the perversions of Cayo and his friends are contrasted and highlighted. Carlota gives details of her past service with Hortensia to the new maid, Amalia. In describing the friends and activities of her mistress, and the wealth of don Cayo, she also provides this information to the reader:

...la señora da muchas fiestas, le dijo Carlota, los amigos del señor eran importantes, había que atenderlos bien (222);

Todas las amigas de la señora son artistas, le dijo Carlota...la señora también había sido artista (240);

¿Era don Cayo muy rico? Carlota abrió los ojazos: riquísimo, estaba en el gobierno, era Ministro. (225)

Amalia, the most recently hired employee, is the first to discover and relate another detail, the lesbian relationship between Hortensia and Queta:

"ahí estaba Hortensia...ahí estaba también la señorita Queta. Parte de las sábanas y del cubrecama se habían deslizado hasta la

103

alfombra, la señorita dormía vuelta hacia ella, una mano sobre la cadera, la otra colgando, y estaba desnuda, desnuda"(251).

Símula's role in the revelation of information is less important, apparently due to natural inclination: "La negra Símula era gorda, canosa, callada" (225). Nevertheless early in the novel, she notes that the object of a political uprising in Arequipa, an event which later becomes an important element in the narrative, is the overthrow of the hated Cayo Bermúdez, and not the removal of President Odría: "Símula encogió los hombros: al que se lo irían a sacar del ministerio era al señor (don Cayo), todos lo odian" (347)

As each member of this chorus reveals fragments of information about the protagonists and the plot of this section of the novel, they also exhibit their own typical behaviors. Amalia, for example, is an openly sensuous figure. During the course of her exchanges with Carlota and Símula she is also slowly succumbing to her own carnal desires. Drawn towards don Cayo's chauffeur, she ultimately is seduced by him. Although she is surprised by the sexual behavior of her mistress Hortensia, she is not repulsed by it. To her, the discovery is more a novelty than a perversion: "En la escalera se echó a reir, llegó a la cocina tapándose la boca, sofocada. Carlota, Carlota, la señorita está ahí en la cama con la señora ... Amalia se mordía la mano para contener las carcajadas"(252-53). Amalia's subsequent seduction by the chauffer Ambrosio thus comes as no surprise, especially since it occurs while she is under the influence of the loose moral atmosphere of don Cayo's San Miguel residence.

Símula is the antithesis of Amalia. Close-mouthed and prudish, "siempre tan seca" (321), she assumes an overly protective mother-role, and closely monitors the curiosity of her daughter and of Amalia as well. She foils the two young girls' attempts to eavesdrop on Hortensia's parties, and censures the younger women's frivolity with sobering refranes.

Carlota, whose desires are repressed by the influence of her mother, floats in constant tension between the liberty that her friend Amalia epitomizes and the reprobation threatened by Símula. Carlota seeks a semblance of freedom with Amalia, but her new friend reveals that these attempts are unsuccessful: "Algunas veces salía con Carlota, pero no muy seguido, porque Símula quería que Amalia le trajera antes del anochecer ... Pobre Carlota, Símula no la dejaba asomar la nariz a la calle" (273).

As individuals, these characters are types, with easily identifiable, one-sided personalities. However, when they are merged in a choral character in order to reveal the ambiance of Cayo Bermúdez household, they also merge psychologically into a single, coherent choral figure. The three aspects of this group character, the facets of instinctual gratification (Amalia), the prohibitive function (Símula), and the tension-filled middle

105

ground (Carlota), combine three essential psychological elements that are traditionally thought to contribute to the dynamics of a single personality: The id, the superego, and the ego.

None of the narrative patterns exhibited by la Orquesta in Casa Verde or the psychological dimensions observed in the servant group in Conversación can be detected in the members of the adolescent chorus that relates the tragedy of Cuéllar in Los cachorros. Apart from distinguishing nicknames, Choto, Chingolo, Mañuco, and Lalo, they manifest few characteristics that would assist in their classification as individuals or distinct types. Although their individual dialogues are sprinkled throughout the text, most of the novel's action is relayed by the ubiquitous collective narrator that shunts back and forth between first and third person plural forms. In Los Cachorros any threads of individuality that could add depth and breadth to the choral character are deliberately attenuated for thematic purposes. The four adolescents mirror each other's behavior so well that they are indistinguishable.

The salient feature of this collective personality is its unequivocal acceptance of the cultural rites of its social class. Each stage of typical adolescent development, from interest in sports and films to girls and dancing is announced, described, and dispensed with in robot-like, unhesitating sequence. The awakening sexuality that triggers such shifts of interest is a

106

universal phenomenon. In the course of following their natural instincts, however, the Cachorros chorus blindly obeys the particular social precepts of its middle class Limeñan milieu. Their collective inability to challenge or question the social code is illustrated in their reaction to the imposition of the obscene nickname, Pichula, on their fellow group member, Cuéllar. Although aware of the sufferings that the apodo causes him, they stifle their misgivings and begin to refer to him as Pichulita: "También a ellos, Cuéllar, que al comienzo nos cuidábamos, cumpa, comenzó a salírseles, viejo, contra nuestra voluntad, hermano..." (67).

Ultimately the psychological and physical effects of Cuéllar's castration preclude his successful adherence to the Cachorros' social code. The group's reaction to this failure is predictable, and includes both the stereotyping and isolation of the individual: "Ya está, decíamos, era fatal: maricón...se le disculpaba, pero, hermano, resulta cada día más difícil juntarse con él ..." (114); "Desde entonces nos veíamos poco ...." (116). After Cuéllar's death, the chorus remains blind to its own role in his suffering and demise: "pobre, decíamos en el entierro, cuánto sufrió, qué vida tuvo, pero este final es un hecho que se lo buscó" (117).

As a choral protagonist epitomizing an entire social class, the Cachorros' commentaries disclose a stunted, conformist group

nature that reflects a "renuncia de la vida auténtica,"[7] in favor of a bland domesticity. The group's final narration, which concludes the work, summarizes and satirizes their staid, homogeneous personality: "Eran hombres hechos y derechos y teníamos todos mujer, carro, hijos...y se estaban construyendo una casita para el verano...y comezábamos a engordar y a tener canas,
barriguitas, cuerpos blandos, a usar anteojos para leer, a sentir malestares después de comer y de beber y aparecían ya en sus pieles algunas pequitas, ciertas arruguitas"(117).

The chorus plays a significant role in Vargas Llosa's early fiction.[8] In the three works discussed here, choral background commentary either summarizes, elaborates upon, or advances plot development. Typically, Vargasllosan choral members are largely unindividuated. Collectively, however, they can possess the psychological dimensions of a protagonist, as do the housemaids in Conversación, or they can communicate the multi-sensory impressions of an observant individual, as does la Orquesta in Casa Verde. A final option, which occurs in Los cachorros, is the representation of the total sublimation of the individual's desires to the ritualized will of the chorus. In this case, the personality of the choral quartet in question highlights and synthesizes the notion of the evils of total class conformity, a theme that pervades the novel.

NOTES

[1]see Luis A. Díez, <u>Vargas Llosa's Pursuit of the Total Novel</u> (Cuernavaca: Centro Intercultural de Documentación, 1970), C.4.

[2]José Miguel Oviedo, <u>Mario Vargas Llosa: la invención de una realidad</u>, 2nd ed. (Barcelona: Barral Editores, 1977) 191.

[3]Díez, C. 4. 23.

[4]Antonio Avaria,"<u>La Casa Verde</u>", Anales de la Universidad de Chile, Año 124, No. 138 (1966):222.

[5]El Arpista previously played an important role in the story as the mysterious don Anselmo, builder of the original Casa Verde.

[6]Avaria 222.

[7]Oviedo 200.

[8]The use of complex choral characters is largely absent in Vargas Llosa's more recent novels. An important exception worthy of further study is the chorus of misfits that isolates and insulates the enigmatic figure of Antonio el Consejero en <u>La guerra del fin del mundo</u> .

Chapter Eight

Rhetorical Digressions

In the Institutio Oratoria, the first-century A.D. Hispano-Roman rhetorician Quintillian defines the figure as a "form of expression to which a new aspect has been given by art."[1] Figures of speech may be further divided into tropes, which involve "a deviation from the ordinary and principal signification of a word, and schemes, which involve a deviation from the ordinary pattern or arrangement of words."[2] Parentheses pertains to the latter subdivision of figures, being a figure of construction that involves the insertion of some verbal unit in a position that interrupts the normal syntactical flow of the sentence. In prose narrative, parentheses may be indicated and set off in many ways, including commas and dashes. This essay will focus on, but not be limited to those occurrences of parentheses that are marked by standard parenthetic brackets.

Since its publication in 1977, critical attention directed to Mario Vargas Llosa's La tía Julia y el escribidor has centered primarily on the presence of humor, irony, and parody in the novel. Overlooked in these analyses is the presence of over 430 parenthetic expressions in the course of the work's 447 pages. Given the fact that such parenthetic proliferation is a hallmark of none of the author's 10 other novels, the average of almost one parenthetic usage per page in _La tía Julia_ merits critical attention. I suggest that parentheses are employed in the novel as part of a deliberate rhetorical, stylistic, and narrative strategy. In addition to contributing to the aforementioned notions of humor, irony, and parody, parenthetic expressions also help to develop plot, add dimensions to character and incident, and supply another narrative voice or layer to the already inherently multi-layered text.

La tía Julia's odd-numbered chapters retrospectively recount events in the life of an eighteen year-old protagonist, Mario Vargas, events that lead to his abrupt elopement with the thirty-two year-old Julia, a distant relative through marriage. Interwoven in this narrative chain of occurrences are accounts that likewise recall the narrator's attempts to become a successful fiction writer, and his close yet improbable friendship with Pedro Camacho, creator of radio soap-operas for Radio Central in the Lima of the mid-1950's. With the exception of Chapter 20, which functions as an epilogue, the even-numbered chapters present prose adaptations of nine distinct radio soap-operas allegedly penned by the prolific Pedro Camacho.

Approximately one-third of La tía Julia y el escribidor's parenthetic expressions occur in the odd-numbered "Mario" chapters. Their average number remains fairly constant in each chapter, and their functions are multiple. The most simple and recurring type of parenthetic expressions in these portions of the text are those that either explain or clarify immediately preceeding statements or those that elaborate upon or restate prior observations. Thus, for example, the narrator, describing his "seance" encounter with a spiritualist bank employee, states that "el escribano nos hizo sentar alrededor de la mesa," adding in parentheses, with reference to the table, "no redonda, sino cuadrangular (70)." These type expressons are often introduced with an explanatory phrase, such as "es decir," "en realidad," "más exactamente," or "más bien." Thus, for example, as Mario relates events that took place when he and his soon-to-be-bride would meet clandestinely, he states, "nos contábamos con lujo de detalles todo lo que habíamos hecho desde la última vez (151)," and then adds in parentheses, referring to the amount of time that they have spent apart, "es decir, algunas horas atrás o el día anterior (151)." Elsewhere Mario asserts that "de vez en cuando la invitaba [a Julia] a almorzar," but then supplies the clarifying parenthetic statement, "más exactamente, los días de pago (150-151)."

It is clear that many such amplification or explanation parentheses serve a dual purpose. Beyond providing simple addenda or clarification, the contrastive nature of many such items with events portrayed in the original stated sentence forms the basis of much of the humor in the novel. In the aforementioned instances, for example, Mario's magnanimous assertion that he used to invite Julia to lunch is humorously tempered by the parenthetic admission that this occurred only on paydays. In like manner, the statement of the lovers' eagerness to see each other after periods of separation is comically modified by the parenthetic observation that such separations usually were for just a few hours. At times, the humor elicited by the contrast between what is stated in the regular narrative and what is affirmed in parentheses abandons any notion of subtlety, and becomes overt. Thus, for example, as the aforementioned spiritualist conjures up the spirit of Mario's dead brother at the young man's request, Mario's surprise is hilariously registered in his parenthetic observation, "porque nunca había tenido hermanos (71)."

Many explanatory/clarification parentheses represent the distanced, reflective and ironic comments of the mature narrator from the perspective of the novel's narrative present. Such comments are often heralded by time expressions that emphasize the temporal distance between then (the era of the events in the

113

novel) and _now_ (the mature narrator's present time). Examples of this type of introductory comment include such phrases as 'Estaba _entonces_ convencido ... (74);" "en _esa edad_ de piedra ... (111);" "como todas las mujeres que había conocido _hasta entonces_ (110);" "Después lamenté esos escrúpulos ... (192)" [All emphasis is mine].

The distancing effect achieved in such parenthetic expressions serves a two-fold purpose. Most obviously, it reiterates the implicit time gap and emotional distance between the narrator and the novel's character of the same name. Such expressions in contrast exercise an opposite effect on the reader by creating a feeling of intimacy with the present-time narrator. In his standard study on rhetoric, Edward Corbett summarizes the relationship created between narrator and reader in parentheses in the following manner: "Although the parenthetical matter is not necessary for the grammatical completeness of the sentence, it does have a pronounced rhetorical effect. For a brief moment we hear the author's voice, commenting, editorializing, and, for that reason, the sentence gets an emotional charge that it otherwise would not have (467)." The total impact of this process in _La tía Julia_ is even more subtle than that mentioned by Corbett. The combined effect of distancing the narrator from his character and at the same time creating "intimacy" with the reader through the parenthetic comments in these instances

114

creates situations of dramatic irony, that is, situations when the narrator and the reader share knowledge that the characters do not hold.

Parentheses is employed in several other important ways in the "Mario" chapters of the novel. On numerous occasions, for example, the parenthetic expressions consist of phrases or sentences in quotation marks that represent the exact, literal, expressed opinions of either Mario or other characters in the novel. In describing a friend and accomplice's encounter with Mario's enraged father after Mario has eloped with Julia, for example, the narrator states, "muerto de pánico, Javier le juró y requetejuró por su madre y por todos los santos que no lo sabía (403)." Javier's literal response to this encounter with Mario's armed father, "hasta ahora sólo había visto revólveres en películas, compadre," is added in parentheses in this portion of the text. Later, the young Mario narrates his attempt to reconcile his mother to his marriage: "Traté de hacerla sonreir, con una broma que resultó de pésimo (409);" he then encapsulates his exact words at that moment in parentheses: "pero mamacita, deberías estar feliz, si me he casado con una gran amiga tuya (409)."

Elsewhere, during an early encounter with Julia, Mario relates that his future wife "jamás había escuchado una radionovela, ni puesto los pies en un teatro desde que interpretó

115

la Danza de las Horas ... el año que terminó el colegio," adding in parentheses Julia's actual afterthought, "no te atrevas a preguntarme cuántos años hace eso, Marito (20)."

The supplemental dialogues represented in these type parentheses in effect recreate a second, dialogic version of the events portrayed in the principal narration - a version that frequently differs with that of the principal narration. They likewise can provide insights into characterologic motivations or preoccupations that are often not apparent in the non-parenthetic text.

Parentheses thus have many functions in the Mario narratives. On an elemental level, they expand or elaborate upon the primary narrative. They also help to establish the humor in the text, and likewise assist in distancing the narrator from the action while creating intimacy with the reader. Finally, they provide supplemental dialogue that gives further insights into plot and character in these segments of the novel.

The nearly 300 remaining parenthetic expressions in La tía Julia are densely concentrated in the nine chapters that represent prose adaptations of Pedro Camacho's radio soap operas. They are noteworthy not only for their multiple functions, but likewise for the manner and frequency in which they appear in the text.

Although many parenthetic expressions in the Pedro Camacho segments repeat the relatively simple and predictable functions of clarification or of providing additional information (functions that we observed in the Mario sections), Pedro's usage of the device offers a different perspective that provides clues to the changing nature of his personality in the novel. Many of his clarifying or elaborating parentheses, for example, represent overt attempts to establish the author's intellectual position, through the use of Latin terms such as <u>dixit</u> (267) and <u>estrictu</u> <u>sensu</u> (216), or the employment of erudite or pedantic vocabulary, as in the phrase "por atractivos cremátisticos (178)." Paradoxically, they reveal at the same time a manic preoccupation with bodily functions, the prurient, the socially unacceptable, or the simply disgusting. Examples of this type parenthetic expression include references to nymphomania (Chapter 8), masturbation (Chapter 6), and abortion (Chapter14), and likewise include such addenda as the description of potions made of "orines propios con ratones macerados (292)."

Midway through the Pedro Camacho narratives, a new parenthetic device, the interrogative phrase, appears, and then reappears with increasing frequency until the end of these narrative sequences. Initially, the parenthetic questions represent the reflections or self-doubts of characters from Pedro's stories. In Chapter 8, for example, in describing the mental dilemma of the exterminator Federico Téllez Unzátegui, who is considering murdering his daughters for having been photographed in bikinis for a magazine, we are informed, "La idea de convertirse en filicida lo atormentaba menos que saber que miles de humanos habían merodeado ...por las intimidades físicas de sus varonas (182)." In the text, the verb "habían merodeado" is followed by Federico's anguished parenthetic query,"¿sólo por los ojos?(182)." Later, in Chapter 10, a series of conflicting interrogative options for the future actions of another protagonist, the drug salesman Lucho Abril Marroquín, are offered in parentheses prior to the resolution of the conflict by the character. By the end of this chapter, however, the interrogative parentheses no longer represent the internal thoughts, conflicts or potential options for the soap opera protagonists, but rather reflect the concerns of their purported author, Pedro Camacho. For example, to the following observation regarding soap opera characters, "Nada, en aparencia...afeaba el marco en el que se desenvolvía la vida de los Abril Marroquín(229)," is appended Pedro Camacho's own parenthetic query regarding "apariencias": "¿pero acaso no recomienda la sabiduría popular no fiarse de apariencias?(229)."

By Chapter 12, the interrogative parentheses give strong indication of increasing uncertainty or confusion on the part of Pedro with regard to his characters or their motivations. By

118

Chapters 14 and 16, Pedro is, in parentheses, regularly confusing setting, events, character names, and even character sexes. This process reaches an apocalyptic crescendo in the last radionovela, and provides clear indication of the strained mental state of the soap operas' alleged creator. Thus, in their functional transformation from representing the thoughts of Pedro's characters to ostensibly representing those of the characters' creator, parenthetic interrogatives provide unexpected insights into character on two different story levels in the novel.

Another stylistic hallmark of the Pedro Camacho parenthetic usages is the increasingly frenetic employment of anticipatory phrases. This technique effectively takes the traditional parenthetic usage and stands it on its ear. The most common function of parentheses -- expansion or elaboration upon a previously stated idea - is here reversed, for the elaboration/expansion is offered to the reader before the concept to which it refers is mentioned in the primary narration.

As in the case of the interrogatory parentheses, the anticipatory parentheses appear first at the approximate midpoint of the Pedro Camacho narratives, and then reappear with increasing frequency until the last serialized saga reaches its conclusion. Some excerpted examples of this process are as follows:

Cuando Lucho Abril Marroquín recobró el sentido estaba en Lima en un cuartito de hospital, fajado de pies a cabeza, y a los flancos de su cama, ángeles de la guarda que devuelven la paz al agitado, mirándolo con inquietud se hallaban la blonda connacional de Juliette Gréco y el Dr. Schwalb ... (214);

... El Padre Seferino Huanca Leyva...había mantenido efectivamente puro, cuando hizo su llegada al barrio de Medocita, serpiente del paraíso que adopta las formas voluptuosas, ubérrimas, llenas de brillos lujuriantes de la hembra, una pervertida que se llamaba Mayte Unzátegui ... (308);

... repite se eres hombre ...--No soy, pero repito --repuso Marimacho. Y, honor de espartana capaz de ir al al hoguera por no dar su brazo a torcer, repitió, enriquecida con adjetivos del arroyo, la mentada de madre. (344) [All emphasis is mine].

In the last use of this technique, in Chapter 18, Pedro is no longer even anticipating the next word or phrase in his parenthetic observations, but rather is jumping ahead and anticipating referents in the next sentence of the text.

A final stylistic hallmark of Pedro Camacho's parentheses, and one that likewise makes its appearance only in the later soap operas, is the abundance of elaborate and often unusual metaphoric language. In Chapter 10, for example, a protagonist's sudden realization is described as a "fogonozo de luz en las tinieblas, lluvia de estrellas sobre el mar (227)." Such poetic comparisons become more frenzied and violent, and less coherent as Pedro's mental confusion increases. Thus, in Chapter 16, for example, Pedro compares the desire of a character to see his son happy and successful to the "debilidades de león que lagrimea viendo a su cachorro despedazar a la primera oveja (341);" and in Chapter 18, the death of two characters is parenthetically compared to "cucarachas que apachurra el zapato (399)." Ultimately, the elaborate metaphors become ridiculous, as in Chapter 16, when a character purports to see certain signs that a woman is beginning to take interest in him, the "señales" he refers to are compared parenthetically to "humo apache en las colinas, tam-tams en la floresta africana (348)."

The effect created by all the above techniques is heightened by the weight of the sheer number of parenthetic expressions, for, as the interrogatory, anticipatory, and metaphorical parentheses become increasingly nightmarish and hallucinogenic, their total number is at the same time increasing almost exponentially chapter by chapter, from a low of two in Chapter 4 to highs of 76 and 67 in Chapters 16 and 18 respectively.

One useful way of summarizing the effect of parenthetic expressions in La tía Julia y el escribidor is to speculate on what would be missed or less-well developed in the novel were the parentheses excluded from the text. In the "Mario" segments, much of the humor would be absent, since a good deal of it is developed by the contrapuntal effect created by the disparity between what is said in the non-parenthetic text and what is said in parentheses. Furthermore, although parentheses are not essential to a basic understanding of the text, much of the richness of events as well as the essential ambiguity of multiple views of characterologic motivation would be lost by eliminating

121

the dialogic parenthetic addendum in the Mario text. Likewise, a good deal of the irony in the novel would be lacking without the frequent, wry, parenthetic observations of the mature narrator on the follies of his youth. Finally, a narrative voice or layer would disappear, since the mature narrator's perspective is actually a double one that consists of the text per se and the parenthetic comments, and since the parenthetic elements are themselves at once a comment on the basic text and its composition as well as a text in their own right.

The Pedro Camacho narrations would also be significantly affected by the elimination of the parentheses. Much of Pedro's own pedantry, obsessions, and hack writing style are revealed in the pauses, interludes, afterthoughts and anticipations that abound in the parenthetic expressions in his soap operas. Perhaps most significantly, in a novel about writers and writing, what better way to describe a literary character's slow descent into insanity than through that character's own stylistic, narrative and rhetorical devices as perceived through the character's own narrative parentheses. Thus, an important metafictional element in the novel would likewise either be greatly reduced or absent in a parentheses-free version of the work.

The extended parenthetic digressions of Mario and Pedro, therefore, represent a unique and essential narrative, stylistic, and rhetorical component in La tía Julia.

NOTES

[1] Marcus Fabius Quintilianus, Institutio Oratoria, trans. H. E. Butler (New York: G. P. Putnam's Sons) IX. i. 14.

[2] Edward P. J. Corbett, Classical Rhetoric for the Modern Student, 2nd ed. (New York: Oxford Univ. Press, 1971) 460.

Chapter 9

The Name Game

Since a fictional protagonist's name is the most obvious and immediate characterological feature to be perceived by a reader, naming commonly has been viewed as the simplest level of characterization[1]. Nevertheless, names and the naming process can also serve more complex functions. The fiction of Peruvian novelist Mario Vargas Llosa reveals an acute sensitivity to such possibilities. This essay suggests that Vargas Llosa utilizes names, nicknames, and the naming process not only as a fruitful method of developmental characterization, but also as a subtle, recurring thematic and structural device.

Vargas Llosa's early novella Los cachorros, traces the history of a young student, Cuéllar, from youth to a premature death. Attacked and emasculated by a dog, the protagonist unsuccessfully fights to main his status in his peer group. The onset of puberty brings predictable problems, difficulties with which Cuéllar is unable to contend. After numerous deliberate encounters with danger, he dies by his own hand in an automobile accident.

124

Early in Los cachorros, Cuéllar, a new student at a Lima colegio, is placed in a group structure where identity is determined almost entirely by nicknames: "en la clase el Hermano Leoncio lo sentó atrás con nosotros en esa carpeta vacía, jovencito. ¿Cómo se llamaba? Cuéllar, ¿y tú? Choto, ¿y tú? Chingolo, ¿y tú? Mañuco, ¿y tú? Lalo" (53). Cuéllar needs a nickname to function within this order and his accident provides one: "Por ese tiempo, no mucho después del accidente, comenzaron a decirle Pichulita. El apodo nació en la clase ..." (65)[2]. Cuéllar initially resists the imposition of his scabrous pseudonym, but ultimately accepts it: "Poco a poco fue resignándose a su apodo" (68). Serious problems associated with his masculinity and with his apodo surface during adolescence when positive female opinions of one's social image become desirable. Like the boys of Cuéllar's neighborhood, the young ladies regularly employ nicknames. Their group consists of figures such as Pusy Lanas, Chabuca Molina, and La China Salvídar. In the girls' eyes, a boy's nickname is an important factor in the impression that he makes. Teresa Arrarte, Cuéllar's favorite, reveals how this attitude has affected her impression of him in her complaint to the protagonist's friends: "Pero por qué tenía ese apodo tan feo, éramos muy malcriados, por qué no le pusieron algo bonito como al Pollo o Baby a Superman, o al conejo Villarán ..." (97).

125

In a world of adolescent pseudonyms, Cuéllar's nickname is distinct, since "it refers to an absence, or at any rate a non-functioning of its anatomical referent"[3] and since it separates and isolates him from the very group to which he desperately wishes to belong. Thus, as Luchting further indicates, "the name, 'Pichula' or 'Pichulita' is ultimately what comes to be the young man's undoing" (58)[4].

Variations on the same idea can be observed in Vargas Llosa's first novel, La ciudad y los perros. In this work, the custom of nicknaming among children is affirmed through allusions to the process in the flashbacks of the adolescents cadets at the Leoncio Prado military academy. Cadet Alberto Fernández's youthful acquaintances, for example, are frequently known only by nicknames: Pluto, Tico, el Bebe. Another cadet, Jaguar, though from a more impoverished background than that of Alberto, observes similar rituals. In a monologue that reveals his youthful love for Teresa before entering the military academy, Jaguar asserts: "Yo conocía de nombre a todas las chicas de su clase, y ella los apodos de mis compañeros y profesores" (177). Intimacy and trust between Jaguar and Teresa are symbolically pledged through the mutual revelation of their onomastic codes.

When the cadets enter their new social environment as perros, or underclassmen, new identities are required. Jaguar, the strongest and most cunning, is exceptional in that he is the

126

only group member who chooses his own mote: "me llamo Jaguar. Cuidado con decirme perro" (50). As a dominant figure, it is Jaguar himself who imposes a deprecatory nickname upon the weakest of the group. Richi Arana: "Me das asco--dijo el Jaguar- No tienes dignidad ni nada. Eres un esclavo" (54). From this point on in the narration, Richi is known almost exclusively by his nickname, el Esclavo. Other cadets, in contrast, receive their new identities through unanimous acclaim. Alberto Fernández's title, el Poeta, for example, is bestowed by his colleagues for his ability to write pornographic stories. The nickname of Cadet Boa stems from physiological attributes that are the antithesis of Cuéllar's in Los cachorros. Recalling how he acquired his apodo, Boa reiterates the popular nature of the procedure: "Nunca se sabe de dónde salen los apodos. Cuando empezaron a decirme Boa me réia y después me calenté y a todos les preguntaba quién inventó eso y todos decían Fulano y ahora ni como sacarme de encime ese apodo, hasta en mi barrio me dicen así" (174).

The power of the name in fixing one's status in the group, as well as in the determination of one's self-image, is dramatically demonstrated by Richi Arana after he has become el Esclavo. Having entered the military academy to become a man, he ultimately finds himself isolated and friendless. Like Cuéllar in Los cachorros, Richi's acceptance of his nickname signals both the abandonment of any hope of successful integration into the

127

group and a total loss of self-confidence: "Ahora ya no tenía es-
peranza ... A él lo conocían de inmediato, tal como era, sin
defensas, débil, un esclavo" (119).

The possible negative effects of nicknames and the
adolescent naming process found in early works such as Los
cachorros and La ciudad resurface in two of Vargas Llosa's later
novels, La guerra del fin del mundo and Historia de Mayta. In the
former work, the character Felicio Pardinas, a gentle, intelligent
youth who was born horribly deformed, is given the pejorative
nickname el León de Natuba because of his acute physical
deformities. The announcement of his verbal dehumanization in
the text is followed immediately by a description of Felicio's
systematic expulsion from the society of Natuba: "... los vecinos
no acabaron nunca de aceptar al león ... La docena de hermanos y
hermanas Pardinas lo evitaban ... Los chicos le tuvieron al
principio miedo y luego, repugnancia. Lo acribillaban a pedradas,
escupitajos e insultos si se atrevía a acercarse a verlos jugar"
(101-102). Like his predecessors, Pichula and el Esclavo, the
imposition of Felicio's deprecatory nickname appears to doom him
almost from the outset; indeed, only the chance intervention of
the mysterious prophet el Consejero prevents Felicio from being
burned at the stake by his neighbors.

The case of Alejandro Mayta in Historia de Mayta is
somewhat reminiscent of Jaguar in La ciudad, for, like his

predecessor, he himself determines the name by which other refer to him. The narrator notes that although many of Alejandro's school friends had Indian features, "el único de nombre indio que yo recuerdo era Mayta" (9). Alejandro's insistence that he be referred to exclusively by his Indian surname and not by his given name is noted as the primary reason that he is harassed and disliked by his peers: "Lo fastidiábamos mucho ... sobre todo, por llamarse Mayta" (9).

What emerges from this examination of adolescent names and nicknames is the concept of a highly ritualized social organization in which a name or a nickname is influential in the determination of one's self-identity and status with a group. In adult social organization, this same principle is also in effect. Prostitutes, for example, form ubiquitous adult groups in Vargas Llosa's fiction. Upon entering the profession, most of them either choose or are assigned new names. In either case, the aliases are acknowledged pseudonyms that establish new identities and mask former ones. Maclovia, one of the prostitutes in Pantaleón y las visitadoras, succinctly summarizes the significance of her new pseudonym: "Maclovia va sólo con el trabajo, tampoco ése es mi nombre, y en cambio, mi nombre de veras van con todo lo demás, por ejemplo, de mis amistades ... Es como si yo fuera dos mujeres, cada una con un nombre distinto" (194).

In adult society, as in its adolescent counterpart, the name that one chooses or is given is often influential in determining one's self-image. Some find their new roles appealing and choose names that point to positive attributes. Such is the case of Luisa Canepa: "A Luisa Canepa ... la violó un Sargento ... La cosa le gustó o qué sé yo ... pero lo cierto es que ahora se dedica al puterío con el nombre de Pechuga" (15). Others, instead of choosing their own names, have new identities bestowed upon them by their employers. Anselmo, the harpist in La Casa Verde, notes that two new prostitutes in the brothel referred to by the novel's title are assigned apodos by their Madame Chunga: "--La Hortensia, la Amapola--dijo don Anselmo--. Qué nombres les pones, Chunguita" (245).

If a prostitute is assigned an apodo that she dislikes, or if the mote is assumed only to mask a former identity, the new name's effect is frequently negative. Bonifacia, who works at Chunga's bar in Casa Verde, does not receive her exotic nickname, La Selvática, from Chunga. Her mote is imposed by the pimp Josefino on the day that her husband is sent to jail in the Lima penitentiary. The imposition of the apodo is repugnant to her: "y por qué me dices Selvática si sabes que no me gusta, ves, ves como eres malo?" (350). Since she cannot follow her husband to Lima, Bonifacia wishes to return to the familiarity of her native province. Josefino, confident that he will be able to use

130

Bonifacia as he wishes, assures her of the impossibility of this plan. Penniless and pregnant, with no other options available, Bonifacia is forced to put herself at the mercy of Josefino. The first indication of her assumption of this new role is the acceptance of the new name, la Selvática. This marks the end of her respectability and the beginning of her career as a prostitute. As la Selvática, she reluctantly aborts her child and joins the whores at Casa Verde, supporting Josefino and herself by her work. At the novel's end, Bonifacia reiterates to Don Anselmo the damaging effect that her assumption of the nickname, la Selvática brought to her: "Aquí todos me desprecian, don Anselmo--dice la Selvática--. Dicen Selvática como un insulto" (427).

Like Bonifacia of _Casa Verde, Olga Arellano Rosaura of Pantaleón is obliged by necessity to assume a nickname. This apodo is adopted as a verbal camouflage in order to hide her Peruvian identity. The narrative reveals that in her youth Olga's great beauty caused the death by suicide of two men who were frustrated in their attempts to express their love for her. One of these was the son of the prefect of Iquitos. This fact led to Olga's expulsion from that city as an undesirable. After a few years' exile in the Brazilian town of Manaos, Olga assumes the alias la Brasileña. This permits the young prostitute to return incognito to her native province in Peru. Commenting on Olga's verbal disguise, Chuchupe, an Iquitan madame, relates: "No la veo desde antes que se fuera a Manaos. Entonces no se llamaba Brasileña, Olguita nomás" (115).

There are recognizable similarities in five of the characters discussed thus far. The adolescents Pichula Cuéllar of Los cachorros, el Esclavo Arana of La ciudad, el León de Natuba from La guerra as well as the adults la Selvática of Casa Verde and la Brasileña from Pantaleón are all representative members of a type character that Northrop Frye identifies as pharmakos, or scapegoat figure. According to Frye, "The pharmakos is neither innocent nor guilty. He is innocent in the sense that what happens to him is far greater than anything he has done provokes ... He is guilty in the sense that he is a member of a guilty society, or living in a world where such injustices are an inescapable part of existence"[5].

The examination of the commonplaces of Vargas Llosa's five scapegoat figures reveals that a peculiar nickname, or an undesired or imposed nickname, often is a basic element that separates each character from his respective group and singles him out as an arbitrarily chosen victim. In the Western world the random victim is epitomized in the figures of Ishmael, whose name has become synonymous with the outcast (Frye 41). In a similar fashion, the apodos el Esclavo, Pichula, el león de Natuba, la Brasileña, and la Selvática suggest that these figures are misfits in their own fictional societies.

In addition to their connotative value, names, titles, and nicknames also carry their own semantic value. When a nickname is substituted for a proper name, as in much of Vargas Llosa's early narrative, the technical and thematic possibilities of the name's denotative nature become greatly enlarged. Vargas Llosa uses names as both cover terms and as signs with their own semantic value in several ways. They serve as organizing principles, as conveyors of tone, and as contributors to verbal irony and parody.

As an organizing principle, nicknames in Vargas Llosa's fiction frequently are used to type secondary characters. For E. M. Forster, flat characters, or types, "in their purest form ... are constructed round a single idea of quality ... the really flat character can be expressed in one sentence"[6]. Upon entering the narration, a type character is recognized "by the reader's emotional eye, not by the visual eye, which merely notes the recurrence of a proper name" (Forster 68).

In Vargas Llosa's narrative, one frequently encounters such as a single idea or quality expressed not in a single sentence, but rather in the very nickname itself. Secondary character nicknames of this variety fall into three categories: I) those that mark physical characteristics, such as el Cojo in the story "El

133

desafío from the collection Los jefes, el Pesado in La Casa Verde, João Grande from La guerra, and Mascarita from El hablador; 2) those that establish animal parallels with the characters, such as Chuchupe (a poisonous snake) in Pantaleón, el León de Natuba in La guerra, or Choto (kid-goat) in Los cachorros; 3) titles that indicate occupation or rank, such as el Teniente in La Casa Verde, and el Hermano in Pantaleón.

Forster finds two advantages in the use of type characters: the ease with which they are introduced and reintroduced in the story, and the ease with which they are recalled by the reader after their introduction (68). In profiting from these advantages, Vargas Llosa's typing also achieves a high degree of economy: A character can be recognized in a word or two: El Pesado; la Peludita. When immediate recognition is evoked through the descriptive nickname, there is a direct relationship between the sign and the signifier. Forster's "emotional eye," which demands an abstract idea for recognition, thus can be bypassed in favor of the "visual eye."

The efficiency of this technique can be observed in the opening scene of Casa Verde, in which a patrol of civil guards from Santa Mariá de Nieva accompanies two nuns in search of young Indian girls:

El Sargento echa una ojeada a la Madre Patrocinio y el moscardón sigue allí. La lancha cabacea sobre las aguas turbias, entre dos murallas de árboles que exhalan un vaho quemante, pegajoso. Ovillados bajo el palmacarí, desnudos de la cintura para arriba, los guardias duermen abrigados por el verdoso amarillento sol del mediodía: la cabeza del Chiquito yace sobre el vientre del Pesado, el Rubio transpira a chorros, el Oscuro gruñe con la boca abierta. Una sombrilla de jejenes escolta la lancha, entre los cuerpos se evolucionan mariposas, avispas, moscas gordas. El motor ronca parejo, se atora, ronca y el práctico Nieves lleva el timón con la izquierda, con la derecha fuma y su rostro, muy bruñido, permanece inalterable bajo el sombrero de paja. Estos selváticos no eran normales, ¿por qué no sudaban como los demás cristianos? Tiesa en la popa, la Madre Angélica está con los ojos cerrados ... (9)

Eight characters are introduced in the original sixteen-line text of the passage. Nicknames and titles help to combat the extreme density of character presentation by assisting in the reader's assimilation of the figures presented. Because of these nicknames, characters are perceived in the mind's eye much as one would gauge a stranger on the street, that is, on the basis of visual signs or surface features, such as a nun's habit, a shock of blond hair, dark skin, or a sergeant's stripes.

This passage also reveals that clusters of characters of similar status often have similar generic nicknames. All the enlisted men are identified by physical traits. The remaining men are distinguished by their rank and profession respectively, while the two women are recognized by their religious titles. The organizing principle of the nickname is thus quite efficient. It first assigns an individual sign to each character, and then organizes groups of characters under generic signs.

Prostitutes represent another class of secondary figures in Vargas Llosa's novels whose apodos assist in the organization of the works in which they appear. Like the soldiers, commanders, and nuns of Casa Verde, they tend to have characteristic generic nicknames. Some have apodos that describe them either figuratively or literally, such as Pies Dorados or la Pechuga. Others are equated with flora or fauna, like La Ranita, la Luciérnaga, and la Amapola in Casa Verde, or Chuchupe and Iris in Pantaleón. A third class, unique to prostitutes, is composed of women who employ forename aliases that have an exotic quality, such as Ivonne in Conversación and Nanette in Los cachorros.

In Pantaleón, the exigencies of plot call for an ever-increasing number of prostitutes. Captain Pantoja's troubles multiply as his euphemistically termed "visitadora" service expands, and more than twenty of the final number of fifty prostitutes are actually introduced in the narrative. At least two-thirds of these have pseudonyms that fit into one of the aforementioned categories. As in the case of the characters in the introductory passage of Casa Verde, generic conformity in the naming process assists in the reader's assimilation of an otherwise prohibitive number of secondary characters.

A name is an attribute; an ambiguous name is an ambiguous attribute. Just as a name can be used to help the reader identify characters quickly, it can also be used to help keep a character deliberately vague. Among both major and minor figures in Vargas Llosa's fiction, a deliberate vagueness in the naming process frequently occurs. At times a conscious blurring of character is achieved by attributing the same name or title to different characters in the same work. Different men, for example, carry the title el Teniente in _Casa Verde_. In the shuffled sequences that comprise the book, no attempt is made to distinguish between the two soldiers. Additionally there are at times two different men who use the title el Sargento. One is a military sergeant, Roberto Delgado. The other is the civil guard, Lituma. They do not become readily distinguishable until Book 3 of the novel, when they both participate in an expedition in search of bandits. Confusion is also fostered by the fact that Delgado is originally introduced as Cabo Delgado.

In _La tía Julia_ Vargas Llosa introduces three different characters with the same first name. El tío Lucho is the narrator's uncle. Lucho Gatica is a "cantante de boleros chileno"(105). Lucho Abril Marroquín is a pharmaceutical salesman who figures prominently in one of Pedro Camacho's radionovelas that are interspersed throughout the novel. Here, the ostensibly real characters, like the narrator's uncle, tío Lucho, tend to become confused with the imaginative creations of Pedro Camacho, thus reiterating the thematic notion of the thin line between fiction and reality. Deliberate onomastic ambiguity is also apparent in the plethora of relatives in the novel that are referred to as "tío" and tía," despite the fact that many are not

137

actually related to the narrator. The use of these terms serves to blur the individual's traits or identity. These members of Mario's "tribu familiar" (105) collectively stand for a position of moral propriety against which the protagonist ostensibly battles. Elsewhere, in Pantaleón, Vargas Llosa uses onomastic similarity to contrast antithetical moral positions in the work in a humorous fashion: "juega la oposición entre dos tipos femeninos, mediante la identidad del nombre: hay dos Leonor: la madre de Pantaleón, y Leonor Curinchila (alias 'Chuchupe'), regenta de prostíbulos, su socia. Una es la 'madre buena,' y otra es 'la madre mala" (Boldori de Baldussi 36).

Roland Barthes has noted that the use of stereotyped forenames in major fictional characters tend to "accentuer la fonction structurale du Nom, déclarer son arbitraire, le depersonaliser"[7]. On the other hand, the use of a patronym, as in "Sarrasine," by Balzac, "C'est prétendre que le substitute patronymique est plein d'une personne (civile, nationale, sociale), c'est exiger que la monnaie appelative soit en or" (102). Although Vargas Llosa's character forenames are not stereotypes, the "ambigüedad antimaniquea"[8] evident in so many of his creations is often enhanced through the assignation of forenames with no accompanying surnames. Lalita and Bonifacia, Anselmo, Aquilino, and Fushía in La Casa Verde and Queta in Conversación are similar in this respect.   There is a mythic side to characters such as

Anselmo and Fushía, two empire builders of the city and the jungle, respectively. Part of the mystery that is evoked by their figures arises from their obscure origins and inscrutable backgrounds; their lack of surnames helps to create this image.

Onomastics also can play a role in establishing the tone of a literary work. Contemporary concern with tone dates from I. A. Richards's use of the term to express a literary speaker's "attitude to his listener"[9]. This attitude, for Richards, is conditioned and conveyed through the author's method of arranging and choosing words. Since nicknames often have their own semantic values, their selective use by the author contributes to the establishment of tone in fiction.

In Vargas Llosa's La ciudad, the nickname of el Esclavo and the animal associations with the names of Boa and Jaguar tend to reinforce the nightmarish society of violence and brutality evident in the work. A similar tone is expressed in the nicknames los jefes, los pajarracos, and los coyotes in the collection of short stories, Los jefes. Throughout the Peruvian writer's early fiction, "La profunda identificación de los personages y Vargas Llosa con las formas de violencia y brutalidad físca se advierte hasta en la fiera jeraquía (zoológica, frecuentemente) a la que son sometidos sus propios nombres: 'jefe,' 'esclavos,' 'perros,' el Jaguar, Boa, La Selvática, los Inconquistables" (Oviedo189). The verbal violence of Pichula Cuéllar's nickname, in Los cachorros, "lo excluye de la normalidad, lo marca para siempre, perpetua y consagra la emasculación"[10]. Equally strong, but more sordid impressions are evoked in Conversación through such nicknames as Bola de Oro (associated with homosexuality in Los cachorros), or the mote of Cayo Bermúdez, whose nickname Cayo Mierda "is also scatalogical: 'Cayo Shithead'"[11] Blended with these forceful terms applied to major characters are a myriad of derogatory terms scattered throughout the dialogues, terms that likewise define the tone of the work: "La novela abunda en estos apodos que dividen--'burgués, 'supersabio,' 'trozkista,' 'maricón'" [12]

Historically, the deliberate use of humorous names has been a persistent practice among novelists. One need look no further than the works of the early masters Cervantes and Fielding to find such characters as Sancho Panza and Rocinante from Don Quijote, Mrs. Slipslop from Joseph Andrews, and Mr. Thwackum from Tom Jones. These protagonists' names contribute to the general tone of mirth that the respective novels display.

In addition to utilizing literary onomastics to produce negative impressions, Vargas Llosa also employs names and motes to enhance the humorous aspect of a work. General Felipe Collazos in Pantaleón, for example, has a nickname, el Tigre, that on the surface "evokes that of another leader, Jaguar" (Oviedo, "Theme" 22). What emerges, however, is a character who is the antithesis of his apodo. Collazos, "jefe de Administración, Intendencia y

Servicos Varios del Ejército" (37), routinely rubber-stamps Pantaleón Pantoja's continued requests for more prostitutes, despite warnings of impending chaos. He expresses little concern over a series of crucifixions perpetrated by a group of religious fanatics. He likewise agrees to such schemes as the distribution of discount coupons to soldiers using the visitadora service. Collazos's bumbling inefficiency and complete lack of initiative thus make his aggressive nickname a total misnomer. The "tiger" is a humorously ironic symbol of bureaucratic ineptitude.

General Collazos's aide is Colonel López López. The Colonel's double surname reflects the common Hispanic custom of formally using the family names of both father and mother. Unless the maternal lineage is exceptional, or the name itself particularly noteworthy, the mother's family name is customarily dropped in normal usage. The fact that Colonel López López's maternal surname is exactly the same as that of his father humorously demonstrates its exceedingly common nature. His continued use of both names adds a ludicrous note to an already comic portrayal.

Humorous wordplay is also evident in the nickname that Pantaleón himself receives, "pan-pan". This gives rise to puns such as "Hay que llamar al pan pan y al vino vino" (82), and to the creation of a new term, Pantilandia, to refer to Pantoja's visitadora command post. Elsewhere, Pantoja's first name becomes the subject of other instances of onomastic manipulation

141

and amusement, as in the comment, "Más pantalones, Pantoja" (289).

Besides satirizing city dwellers like Collazos and López López, Vargas also takes playful aim at the country bumpkins who inhabit the villages surrounding Iquitos. Castro-Klarén has noted that among the lower-class people of this region there appears to be a tradition of using colorful and, at times, humorous names[13]. Vargas Llosa frequently avails himself of this tradition in Pantaleón. One of Pantoja's Indian helpers, for example, is named Sinforoso Caiguas. Sinforoso has connotations of hollowness, and a caigua is a gourdlike vegetable native to Peru. Similar in nature are the names of three of la Brasileña's violators. Nepomuceno Quilca's forename is an archaic reference to an obscure saint. Altidoro Soma's patronym is a term for a type of coarse flour. Caifas Sansho's first name is the same as that of the Jewish priest who condemned Christ to death; his last name is a corruption of Sancho, an appellation that is charged with quixotic implications.

In Pantaleón, therefore, the names of many characters frequently "suenan como las carcajadas que producen" (Oviedo, Mario Vargas Llosa 275). The "comicidad implícita en la ironía de los nombres"[14] contributes significantly to the humorous tone of the work.

The conscious employment of humorous names evident in Vargas Llosa's first comic novel, Pantaleón, is continued in La tía Julia. Here, minor figures are dubbed with such names as el Negro Humilla, Choclo Roman, and Señora Agradecida. Another figure, Doctora Lucía Acémila, felt so much pride in her patronym (which means "mule") that "lo arrojaba como una hazaña, en tarjetas impresas, o en los rótulos de su consultorio, a la visión de los mortales" (216-17).

In addition to their role in the establishment of tone, nicknames also assist in the creation of verbal irony, which arises from "the disparity between the author's words and what he really means"[15]. The use of ironic nicknames presents a highly economical means of conveying verbal irony. In Vargas Llosa's fiction, for example, Alberto Fernández's nickname, el Poeta, in La ciudad, is highly ironic, since it is a title earned through the writing of pornography. In La tía Julia, a name is used to evoke romantic irony, "a mode of dramatic or narrative writing in which the author builds up artistic illusion, only to break it down by revealing that he, as artist, is the arbitrary creator of his characters and their actions" [16]. This effect is produced when the reader discovers that the narrator's name in the novel, Mario Vargas, is the same as the author's.

Bonifacia's nickname, la Selvática, in the novel Casa Verde represents a complex use of verbal irony. Her apodo carries connotations of rustic simplicity that obviously clash with the realities of her profession as a prostitute. As a young convent intern , Bonifacia exhibited this naiveté in her release of the young Indian girls captured by the nuns. This act of kindness is the first link in a chain of events (expulsion from the convent, marriage to Lituma, trip to Piura, prostitution in the Casa Verde) that again leads her nominally to assume the role of a rustic through her apodo, la Selvática. In the brothel, however, the exotic nickname serves only as an onomastic enticement for her clientele.

In Conversación, the character Hortensia has a pseudonym, la Musa, that is also charged with ironic connotations. Prior to her involvement with the political strongman Cayo Bermúdez, she was a torch singer of considerable renown in Lima: "Ella había sido famosa ... en el escritorio sacó un album de recortes. ... Se los iba mostrando, orgullosa: en traje largo, en ropa de baño, con peinados altísimos, en un escenario de Reina echando besos. Y oye lo que decían los periódicos ... era linda, tenía una voz tropical, cosechaba éxitos" (454). Nevertheless, when la Musa tries to resume her career after her hiatus as Hortensia, she never is able to regain her prior status. The only Musa that the reader knows is the drug-addicted petty prostitute who is brutally murdered. The disparity between her nickname and her true status thus contributes to the ironic portrayal of her character.

An unusual fictional process that is evident in the works of contemporary writers such as William Faulkner, Günter Grass, and Gabriel García Márquez is the practice of reviving characters from one work for use in another. Oscar Matzerath, for example, appears as the dwarf hero of Grass's _The Tin Drum_ and reappears in other works such as _Dog Years_ and _Cat and Mouse_ as a marginal figure. Quentin Compson is a young boy in Faulkner's _Absalom! Absalom!_, and he appears as a suicidal Harvard student in _The Sound and the Fury_. Vargas Llosa, like Faulkner, Grass, and others, utilizes this technique in his fiction, although at times little is left of the original character but the name. Sergeant Lituma, for example, appears as a minor figure in "Un visitante" a story from _Los jefes_. He is a major character in _Casa Verde_, resurfaces briefly in _Historia de Mayta_, appears in multiple roles in _La tía Julía_ and is a major character in _¿Quién mató a Palomino Molero?_ Lalita, a lover of three men in _Casa Verde_, is the lover of many more as a prostitute in _Pantaleón_. Chunga, the male "second" to _el Cojo_ in the story "Un desafío," resurfaces as the daughter of Anselmo in _Casa Verde_ and as a laconic bar owner in _Palomino Molero_.

Vargas Llosa propels the idea of recurring fictional characters into the realm of self-parody in _La tía Julía_. Lituma, familiar to the reader because of his appearances in other works, appears in this novel as a fictional creations of the radionovela dramatist, Pedro Camacho. As the overworked Camacho moves progressively toward insanity, the figure of Lituma begins to jump erratically from one soap opera to another. He is alternately a civil guard, a guard captain who commits suicide at a soccer game, an ex-sergeant curandero, and, ultimately, a nun, Madre Lituma. One of the actors in the radio romances reveals yet another incarnation: "Hipólito Lituma siempre fue un sargento, terror del crimen en el Callao, en el radioteatro de las diez. Pero hace tres días resulta ser el nombre del juez de las cuatro, y el juez se llamaba Pedro Barreda" (283). Mario Vargas, the narrator, whimsically explains this narrative tactic of his friend Camacho: "a lo mejor esos trueques y enredos eran una técnica original suya de contar historias" (242).

At this juncture, the reader enters the Borgesian realm of fiction about fiction. Vargas Llosa, the novelist with a penchant for placing fictional characters from one novel into another, has created a fictional writer, Pedro Camacho, who does the same with one of Vargas Llosa's own characters, Lituma. At the same time, the novelist has devised a fictional character, appropriately named Mario Vargas, who explains this process to the reader. Character and author names are used to show how literature loops back on itself. John Barth's description of this technique in the works of Jorge Luis Borges aptly summarizes such a use of character and onomastics in Vargas Llosa's La tía Julia: "His artistic victory, if you like, is that he confronts an intellectual dead end and employs it against itself to accomplish new human work" [17]

In Vargas Llosa's fictional universe, a protagonist's name can signify more than its sound. The employment of nicknames affords a wider range of connotative and denotative possibilities than the simple name provides. Vargas Llosa's characters frequently demonstrate the significance of apodos in the establishment of their own self-image, and in the determination of their status within social groups. The imposition of a depreciatory nickname often identifies individuals as archetypal scapegoat figures. The careful use of onomastics also serves other thematic and technical purposes. As an organizing principle, the nickname is an efficient method of typing secondary characters, since it frequently projects a precise visual image that assists in the reader's immediate recognition of the figure in question. Contrastively, names and titles can also create deliberate characterological ambiguity. Nicknames thus become verbal masks that temporarily conceal a character's complex personality from the reader or from other protagonists. Additionally, nicknames that convey tones of violence, humor, irony, and parody establish their bearers as emblematic manifestations of the author's thematic concerns.

Throughout his fiction Vargas Llosa employs a simple verbal tool, the name or nickname, to animate, personalize, and epitomize his protagonists, to challenge and engage the reader in the creative process, and to link character symbolically to theme.

NOTES

[1]René Wellek and Austin Warren, Theory of Literature (New York: Harcourt, 1956) 219.

[2]José Miguel Oviedo, in Mario Vargas Llosa: la invención de una realidad (Barcelona: Barral, 1977)118, notes that in Peru, "la palabra Pichula, que designa el sexo masculino, es impronunciable".

[3] Wolfgang Luchting, "Literature as a Negative Participation in Life: Vargas Llosa's Los cachorros/Pichula Cuéllar, World Literature Today, 52 (1978): 58.

[4]Luchting 58.

[5]Northrup Frye, Anatomy of Criticusm, 3rd ed. (Princeton: Princeton UP) 43.

[6] E.M. Forster, Aspects of the Novel, (New York: Harcourt, n.d.) 67-68.

[7]Roland Barthes, S/Z, (Paris: Seuil, 1970) 102.

[8] Carlos Fuentes, La nueva novela latinoamericana (Mexico, D.F.: Mortiz, 1969)36.

[9] I. A. Richards, Practical Criticism (New York, Harcourt, n.d.)175.

[10] José Emilio Pacheco, "El contagio de la culpa," in Asedios a Vargas Llosa, ed. José Emilio Pacheco et al (Santiago: Editorial Universitaria, 1972): 14

[11] José Miguel Oviedo, "The Theme of the Traitor and the Hero: On Vargas Llosa's Intellectuals and the Military," World Literature Today, 52 (1978): 21.

[12] Jean Franco, "Lectura de Conversación en la Catedral, Revista Iberoamericana, 37 (1971): 764.

[13] Sara Castro-Klarén, "Humor and Class in Pantaleón y las visitadoras, Latin American Literary Review, 7 (1978): 65.

[14] Rosa Boldori de Baldussi, Vargas Llosa: un narrador y sus demonios, (Buenos Aires: García Cambeiro, 1974) 87.

[15]George McMurray, " The Absurd, Irony and the Grotesque in Pantaleón y las visitadoras, World Literature Today, 52 (1978): 46.

[16] M. H. Abrams, A Glossary of Literary Terms, (New York: Holt, 1957) 83.

[17]John Barth, "The Literature of Exhaustion," in On Contemporary Literature, ed. Richard Kostelanetz (New York: Avon, 1969): 668.

Chapter Ten

A Sense of Place

Despite the generally accepted critical notion[1] that poets and novelists regularly use place to convey a wide variety of ideas and attitudes, serious consideration of the role of place in literature has not been the object of much recent critical attention. In 1984, Leonard Lutwack suggested that such a state of affairs may be changing, for

As interest in the social and intellectual contexts suffers from the general disorientation of our time and as the kind of reductionism long practiced in science becomes more popular in the humanities, we can expect criticism to look more closely at the physical contexts within a literary work, specifically, its renderings of space, motion, things, processes and places.[2]

Mario Vargas Llosa's narrative provides a substantial testing ground for this type of critical incursion. The preferred locus of his novels is his native Peru -- from mountain village of northern desert town to Amazon lowlands and the streets of Lima. The titles of several of his novels, such as La ciudad y los perros, La Casa Verde, and Conversación en la Catedral, further hint at the importance of place in his fiction. The author's major novel placed outside of Peru, La guerra del fin del mundo, is, in the same fashion as the Peru novels, inextricably linked to a specific place, the remote settlement of Canudos in Northeastern Brazil.

Numerous critics have noted the general importance of place and geography in Vargas Llosa's novels. John Brushwood, commenting on La ciudad,'s primary settings, Lima and the Leoncio Prado Military Academy, indicates that here "Vargas Llosa creates a world, presents a problem, develops interesting characters, and works out a denouement that holds the reader in suspense."[3] Referring to both Conversación and La guerra del fin del mundo, Dick Gerdes notes that Vargas Llosa has "been known for his ability to present the whole social milieu of a society, be it contempprary urban or rural nineteenth-century Brazil."[4] Raymond L. Williams, commenting on the choral narrator in Los cachorros, states that the novella presented a "technical challenge to the author. Vargas Llosa wanted to tell a boy's story, but the problem was who would tell it. He found his answer in the barrio."[5] Marvin A. Lewis, in his study of how Vargas Llosa views and interprets different periods in Peruvian history, appropriately emphasizes the importance of place in his title: From Lima to Leticia: The Peruvian Novels of Mario Vargas Llosa.[6]

Despite the frequency of such assertions, there have been few detailed analyses of the role of place in Mario Vargas Llosa's fiction, and none have been undertaken utilizing the formal framework of a rhetoric of place, such as the model proposed by Lutwack. By referring specifically to two to the author's works of the 1980's, ¿Quién mató a Palomino Molero? and Historia de Mayta, this essay will suggest first that place in Vargas Llosa's fiction has a sufficiently important influence on the primary interest in the novels in question to merit critical attention. A careful anaysis will then reveal how place interacts dynamically with plot, structure, and character in these works. For the purposes of this essay, place in a literary work is defined as "the reconstitution in words of those aspects of the actual environment that a writer puts together to make up the 'world' in which his characters, events, and themes have their show of existence" (Lutwack 37).

Although the preliminary reception by some critics of Palomino Molero was unenthusiastic,[7] others disagreed, finding that Vargas Llosa's first incursion into the detective sub-genre "genera una serie de cuestiones tan interesantes como sútiles que parecen haber pasado desapercibidas por muchos críticos vargasllosianos"[8]

The action in the novel takes place on the northern Peruvian coast in the mid 1950's. Two Civil Guards, Lituma and Teniente Silva, are attempting to discover the identity and motives of the murderer(s) of a young air force cadet, Palomino Molero. Their investigation leads them to suspect the cadet's superior officer,

151

Colonel Mindreau, and a young lieutenant, Dufó. Further complications include the suspicion of incest on the part of Mindreau, the discovery that his daughter, Alicia, was having an affair with Palomino, and the Colonel's suggestion that Alicia is mentally unbalanced. When it appears that the Civil Guards have solved the crime and implicated Mindreau and Dufó, Mindreau kills his daughter and then commits suicide. Ironically, neither the military nor the townspeople believe the "official" explanation of the crimes offered by Silva and Lituma. The Civil Guards are then inexplicably reassigned to an isolated outpost elsewhere in the country, and, at novel's end, neither the intrepid investigators, the townspeople, nor the reader have the definitive answer to the question posed by the novel's title.

The specific geographic focus of Palomino Molero is the province of Piura, situated on the northern border with Ecuador. Palomino is murdered in an isolated pedregal an hour's walk from the coastal town of Talara, where the Civil Guards are based. Apart from two segments of the novel that take place in the nearby city of Piura and town of Amotape, the plot develops in Talara. Significantly, this coastal fishing town and off-shore petroleum drilling center is provided with a tri-level geographic focus in the novel. High above lies a "zona reservada," "donde estaban las oficinas y las casas de los gringos de la International Petroleum Co."(7). In this isolated and protected region, "detrás de sus muros y rejas vivían [los gringos] igual que en las películas"(35). Beneath this level, but still above that of the town, lies the air base commanded by Colonel Mindreau. Lituma's description of the base upon his first visit there to question Mindreau succinctly describes this area while also revealing Lituma's resentment at the good fortune of the aviators:

> Mientras esperaban Lituma echó una ojeada al contorno. ¡Puta, qué lecheros! ¡Vivir y trabajar en un sitio así! A la derecha se alineaban las casas de los oficiales, igualitas, de madera, empinadas sobre pilotes, pintadas de azul y blanco, con pequeños jardines de geranios bien cuidados y rejillas para los insectos en puertas y ventanas (33)

Physical descriptions of Talara, the town below, contrast sharply with the luxury, order, and comfort of both the gringo zone and the air base:

> En una de las casas de madera unas mujeres abrían los pescados y les sacaban diestramente las vísceras...alrededor brincaban los perros esperando los residuos. Olía fuerte y mal ... había viejos en camiseta sentados en las escaleras, niños desnudos recogiendo conchas ...(121);
>
> No eran aún las ocho y ya el sol quemaba ... el mar estaba cerquita ... el mar de Talara andaba siempre impregnado de residuos de petróleo y de las suciedades de los barcos del puerto ...(29);
>
> Siempre olía a pescado en Talara, pero ciertas noches, como ésta, el olor aumentaba hasta volverse insoportable ....(121)

Within this fetid, unpleasant general environment, further detailed descriptions of specific Talaran settings in which a good deal of the novel's action develops serve to intensify the sense of poverty, disrepair, and seediness associated with the lowest

153

level of the novel's symbolic setting. Doña Adriana's fonda, for example, where the Civil Guards eat and ruminate on the murder case, is described as "una débil armazón de cañas, esteras, y calaminas, con ... unas mesitas chuecas...."(26). Worse yet is the state of the police station, a "casita ruinosa y despintada" (168), despite the efforts of Teniente silva to have it repaired:

El Teniente Silva mandaba oficio tras oficio a la Dirección General de la Guardia Civil, explicando que si no hacían algo pronto se les caería encima y que los calabozos eran una colada de donde los prisioneros no se escapaban por la conmiseracieon o cortesía, pues las tablas de las paredes estaban apolilladas y roídas por los ratones. (168)

The description of a third location, el peñón de los cangrejos, where Teniente Silva and Lituma spy on Doña Adriana and where they receive an important visit from Alicia Mindreau, also merits special attention. At this site, thousands of crabs have hollowed-out caves in the sandy soil. The helter-skelter movements of the crabs in their habitat prompts Lituma to note a parallel between the animals and himself and Teniente Silva: "los vio asomar...era imposible saber si avanzaban o retrocedían. <<Igual que nosotros en lo de Palomino Molero >>, pensó" (110). He likewise associates this surrealistic landscape with danger and horrific possibilities for himself and Teniente Silva:

Se le ocurrió que el cerro entero estaba horodado por las galerías excavadas en él por los cangrejos. ¿Y si, de pronto, cedía? El Teniente Silva y él se hundirían en unas profundidades oscuras, arenosas y asfixiantes, pobladas de enjambres de estas costras vivientes, artilladas con pinzas. Antes de perecer, tendrían una agonía de pesadilla. (111)

In light of the weight of such detailed negative images associated with Talara, it is not surprising that the descent into it from a higher level very nearly acquires for Lituma the symbolism of a Dantesque descent into hell: "La carretera serpenteaba lentamente, descendiendo a Talara por un terreno ocre, sin una sola mata verde, entre pedruscos y rocas de todas las formas y tamaños...El pueblo era una mancha lívida y metálica allá abajo, junto a un mar plomizo, sin olas"(46).

The physical contrasts between Talara's three levels are further enhanced and emphasized by the implicit limitations imposed on those ascending or descending from one level to another. The gringos of the upper zone have no physical presence in the novel, and apparently rarely leave the isolation of their mountain foritification. Only two individuals from the lower levels are permitted to penetrate this safety zone. Don Jerónimo, Talara's lone taxi driver, is allowed entry because he provides the gringo's with an occasional needed service. The second individual, Alicia Mindreu, is allowed on one occasion to use the gringo's swimming pool while the air base pool is being refilled, evidently because of her father's status as base commander and because she is "gente decente" (125). Neither the gringos nor the local Talarans have any access to the middle zone air base.

155

Cadets from the base, however, frequent the town's house of prostitution. Despite the fact that the gringos never descend to the depths of Talara, their symblic presence there is ubiquitous:

... a sus espaldas ... tenían la bahía con sus dos muelles, la refinería erizada de tubos, escaleras y torreones metálicos ...(109);

Sonó la sirena de la refinería y el gallinzo alzó la cabeza y se agazapó ...(177);

El mar de Talara andaba siempre impregnado de residuos de petróleo ....(129)

The effect created by the deliberate differentiation and disparity of physical and atmospheric properties of each of Talara's three levels, and the concept of priviledged vertical accessibility, are reinforced at three critical moments in the novel by the repeated reassertion of the existence of such a tri-level focus. Early on, after Palomino Molero's murder has been discovered, Lituma observes that "gringos y aviadores podían mirarse la cara por sobre las cabezas de los talareños, que se asaban de calor allá abajo en el pueblo, apretado a orillas de un mar sucio y grasiento"(34) As the pieces of the murder-mystery begin to fit together, and as Teniente Silva questions Alicia Mindreau regarding her relationship with Palomino Molero, the Talaran layer-cake geography is again reviewed: " en la cumbre del peñón...donde estaba las casas de los gringos...ya se habían prendidio los postes de luz...también allá arriba de los adcantilados...en la Base Aérea" (122). Finally, in the chapter that

156

ends with Colonel Mindreau's suicide, and as Lituma and Silva discuss the case with a local fisherman, the disparity between the lowest and the highest levels is again reviewed: "La luna alumbraba la noche de tal modo que se veía muy claro, el pérfil de las casas de los gringos...en la cumbre del peñón, junto al faro pestañeante y las faldas del promontorio que cerraba la bahía"(147).

As has been suggested, Palomino Molero's straightforward plot consists of three movements: the discovery of Palomino's murder, the investigation of the crime, and the "resolution" of the situation. If, as Lutwack observes, "Plot is a map of a story's physical environment as well as the pattern of its events"(66), it is clear that the structure of events in this work is deliberately and consciously supported and paralleled by the arrangement of place in the narrative.

Viewed metaphorically, Talara's geography assumes equal importance. In Dante's prototypical three-part geography in the The Divine Comedy, "the physical context of the poem, including the downward and upward movement of the travellers, is a vast metaphor supporting the ethical, philosophical, and religious superstructure of meaning" (Lutwack 66). Such symblism is also present in Palmino Molero, albeit on a less grandiose scale. Economic and political power in Talara and its environs are concentrated in the orderly, peaceful, and climactically and aesthetically pleasant *zona reservada* and air base. These upper levels are either the exclusive domain of whites, or controlled by "non-*cholo*" Peruvians with atypical Hispanic names, such as Mindreau and Dufó. Crime, disease, unhealthy living and working conditions, and racial mixtures are relegated exclusively to the lower sphere. Within this microcosm of Peru, however, the relationship of moral and ethical behavior to sphere or level is the inverse of that displayed in Dante's work, for, in *Palomino Molero*, the higher realms are reserved for the indifferent gringos or the "*peces gordos*, who function outside the law, and the corrupt and perverted military, as epitomized by Colonel Mindreau. In the unattractive nether regions dwell the hard-working and decent folk, such as Doña Adriana, her fisherman-husband, Matías, and Civil Guard Lituma. Thus, in contrast to Dante, the lower one moves in Talara, the higher the propensity for moral rectitude and ethical behavior.

The relationship of character to place in the novel is significant, particularly in the case of Lituma. On a simple level, "the place inhabited by a person ... is ... a sign representing the type of person he is and his function in the story" (Lutwack 69). Within the metaphoric multi-level framework established above, Lituma, the only main character who is a native of the province of Piura, is a representative of the *cholo* lower-class population of the lowest sphere of Talara. In his case, however, the link

158

between place and character is more subtle, for much of the description of place in the novel is either directly or indirectly filtered through him to the reader. The first descriptions of the air base and the description of the peñón de los cangrejos, for example, are, as was indicated previously, made by Lituma. In other instances, such as in the description of the fish odor in Talara, although Lituma himself is not responsible directly for the description, an account of his response to the description immediately follows the description itself: "... ciertas noches, come éstas, el olor [de pescado] aumentaba, hasta volverse insoportable. Lituma sintío una especie de vértigo. Caminó un rato tapándose con el pañuelo"(75). In a final technique of this type, the description of a place is neither a simple association with Lituma nor his own realistic description, but rather, his imagined physical description of it: "Hasta tenían piscina, ahí, detrás de las casas. Lituma nunca la había visto pero se la imaginó llena de señoras en ropa de baño ... "(33, my emphasis).

Such a blend of character and place produces interesting results. We derive a preliminary notion of Lituma as a charcter from the level of Talara that he inhabits. We derive a more complex notion of his character from his own subjective descriptions or imagined descriptions, or through indirect association of places with him. At many points in the novel, then, the reader's sole perception of place derives from a character's impressions of it. At the same time, such descriptions provide us with insights into the psychological, emotional, and ethical dimensions of Lituma the character. In such instances, then, place becomes an integral component of character, and character an integral component of place.

A final irony of <u>Palomino Molero</u> that definitively links character to place involves the concept of displacement. In the three-tiered hierarchy and upside-down value scheme of Talara, Lituma's honest search for justice on behalf of Palomino is "rewarded" by his uprooting and dislocation from his native place to a distant, unknown, and undesirable location:

> Malas noticias para ti --dijo el Teniente...--Te han transferido a un puestecito medio fantasma, en el departamento de Junín...ya ves...tanto que querías aclarar el misterio de Palomino Molero...y qué ganamos: que te mandan a la sierra, lejos de tu gente...así se agradan a los buenos trabajos...¿Qué va a ser de ti allá? (188-89)

A hint at the answer to this question is actually provided in the second novel dealt with in this study, <u>Historia de Mayta</u>, a work whose publication chronologically preceded that of <u>Palomino Molero</u> by two years. Late in <u>Mayta</u>, brief mention is made of the two Civil Guards from <u>Palomino Molero</u>, who are now in Junín: "antes de una hora de los sucesos, estaba llegando a Jauja el autobús de Huancayo con una compañía de guardias civiles al mando de un Teniente apellidado Silva y un Cabo de nombre Lituma"(278).

Historia de Mayta, one of the author's darkest meditations on his native Peru, relates on one level the tale of a revolutionary, Mayta, and his attempt to begin an armed rebellion near the Andean town of Jauja in 1958. The events are loosely based on an actual occurence that took place in 1962. On a second level, the reader is introduced to a novelist-narrator strongly resembling Vargas Llosa, who, in the narrative present, is in the act of reconstructing the events of the Jauja rebellion by conducting a series of interviews with those who knew or were associated with Mayta at the time of the actual incident. In the course of his narration, the narrator explains his method: "... no pretendo escribir 'la verdadera historia de Mayta'... Sólo recopilar la mayor cantidad de datos y opiniones sobre él, para, luego, añadiendo copiosas dosis de invención, construir algo que será una versión irreconocible de lo sucedido"(93). A final twist is then applied to the layers of the text. In the alleged "reality"of the apocalyptic narrative present (1984), Peru is in the throes of a civil war, and is being invaded simultaneously from the south by Cuban-Bolivian guerrillas, and from the north by U. S. Marines.

As in the case of Palomino Molero, place in this novel interacts dynamically with theme, plot, and character. Although the narrator announces that the "episodio central" of the novel deals with Mayta's failed uprising in Jauja, "la historia ésa de Jauja" (320), only three of the work's ten chapters actully take

161

place in the Andean town. The events of the remaining seven chapters are placed in Lima, either of the 1950's, or the imagined present of the mid-1980's.

Commenting on the tone of Mayta, Oviedo observes that "Todo está dominado por un aire de asfixia, desesperanza, y fealdad."[9] This pessimistic ambience derives in large part from a continued barrage of negative descriptions of Lima. Within this environment, the ominous present is continually contrasted unfavorably with the admittedly bad conditions that existed in the 1950's, conditions that prompted Mayta's rebellion. This change from bad to worse, even in the "distritos residenciales y privilegiados," is noted on the novel's first page: "son feas estas casas ... son feas estas basuras que se acumulan detrás del bordillo del Malecón y se desparraman por el acantilado"(7). After this observation, the first link between place and human reponse to it in the novel is then postulated: "Si uno vive en Lima, tiene que habituarse a la miseria y a la mugre o volverse loco o suicidarse"(8).

Although the narrator's interviews take him to vastly different sections of Lima, the contrast between then (bad), and now (worse) is omnipresent. Mayta's old neighborhood, formerly a lower-middle class district of "sastres, zapaterías, imprentas" has changed for the worse: "ahora estas calles antaño hamponescas y prostibularias son también marihuaneras y

162

coqueras," having become a neighborhood of "atracos calle-jeros"(15). The streets of the narrator's boyhood neighborhood, formerly a middle-class stronghold, are now "atestadas de patrullas policiales ... hay una ametralladora a la entrada de la Diagonal, protegida por sacos de arena ..."(43). Lima's barriadas, or slums, whose miserable conditions contributed to Mayta's conversion to Marxism, are now even worse: Las cosas han empeorado mucho ... las barriadas han proliferado, a la miseria y el desempleo, se ha añadidio la matanza" (78); "en esta Lima marginal antes había sobre todo la pobreza. Ahora hay, también, sangre y terror" (61). In the Plaza Bolivar, the narrator observes the "gente humilde, "con ropas pobres y algo ridículas ..."(119), who, nevertheless, because they have some meager form of employment, are "grandes privilegiados si se les compara...con esos cholitos descalzos ... o con esa familia de andrajosas" (119). Even the halls of Congress are not immune, for in recent weeks, there have been "dos atendados en el interior del Congreso, uno de ellos muy serio: una carga de dinamita que estalló en Senadores con un saldo de dos muertos y tres heridos" (115).

In sum, the description of all sectors of the city, regardless of social or economic status, is the same vision of an Orwellian urban landscape that is either dead, dying, or under seige. Such a vision has a powerful symbolic value: "Since the city has often served in the history of literature as a symbol of the civilized world in its glory, the destruction of the city is a familiar image in modern apocalyptic writing to represent the fall of civilization"(Lutwack 234).

Although the city does not fare well in this analysis, the narrator, in his journeys to the Andean regions in the the three chapters of the novel not set in Lima, comes to an equally pessimistic view of life in the countryside when speculating on Mayta's response to the living conditions of the mountain peasants:

> ... así serían todas las casitas de Quero: ni luz, ni agua corriente, ni desagües, ni baños. Las moscas y los piojos y mil bichos serían parte del ínfimo mobiliario... en esta mugre, en este desamparo vivían millones de peruanos, entre orines y excrementos, sin luz ni agua, llevando la misma vida vegetativa, la misma rutina embrutecidora ....(282)

Finally, it is the effect of an impression received by the narrator at a symbolic place, the Museum of the Inquisition, in Lima, that provides him with a significant realization about his native city and country. On the site of the inquisitional torture chambers, he realizes that violence has been an invariable ingredient in the history of Peru. As he prepares to leave, he is accosted by beggars. This encounter leads to the following observation: "La violencia detrás mío y delante el hambre. Aquí en estas gradas, resumido mi país. Aquí tocándose, las dos caras de la historia peruana" (124). In this brief passage, past and present are not merely time periods, for, through the powerful geographic presence of the Palace of the Inquisition, they likewise become linked to place.

In the final pages of Palomino Molero, the symbolic displacement of the honest Lituma-- his forced transfer from his native province to a remote region -- provided a further ironic dimension to the novel. In the final chapter of Mayta, the ex-revolutionary, having lost hope in his country, reveals to the narrator that he now feels that in his opinion, such a displacement would be preferable to staying in Peru. The surprised narrator comments on this wish:

Echaste la esponja, ¿no? Piensas o actúas como si lo pensaras, que esto no cambiará nunca para mejor, sólo para peor. Más hambre, más odio, más opresión, más ignorancia, más barbarie. También tú, como tantos otros, sólo piensas ahora en escapar antes que nos hundamos del todo....(337)

As in the case of Palomino Molero, the relationship between place and character in Mayta is significant, since in both works a good deal of what the reader learns about place is presented through the impressions of a character in the work. Lituma served this function in Palomino Molero; in Mayta, this role is assigned to the narrator-novelist. As with Lituma in Palomino, part of our impression of the narrator as character in Mayta is determined by his many observations on the places in and at which he finds himself. Nevertheless, as Wayne Booth asserts, a description of facts provided by an author or unequivocal spokesperson can be very different when given to us by a character in the narrative: "Whenever a fact, whenever a narrative summary, whenever a description must or even might serve as a clue to an inerpretation of the character who provides it, it may very well lose some of its standing as fact, summary, or description."[10] In Mayta, this dilemma is somewhat diminished in Chapter Ten, when ther narrator steps out of his "character" role and (presumably) establishes himself as Booth's unequivocal spokesperson. Here he admits that he is responsible for some "non-factual" aberrations in the first nine chapters, such as the portrayal of Peru as a country invaded by foreign troops, and the portrayal of Mayta as a homosexual. Nevertheless, in the main, the portrait that this "reliable" narrator offers of Lima, specifically the horrific "real" atmosphere of the Lurigancho prision (where he goes in search of the "real" Mayta), is remarkably similar to that presented by the "unreliable" narrator-author in the previous chapters. What, then, is the reader to make of this multi-layered concoction?

In reviewing the central events from both novels, the murder of Palomino Molero, and the tale of Mayta's rebellion, one is struck by the inconsistencies and by a lack of a definitive version of events. Such ambiguity, evident in Teniente Silva's advice to Lituma: "nada es fácil, Lituma. Las verdades que parecen más verdades, si les das muchas vueltas, si las miras de cerquita, lo son a medias o deja de serlo" (107), is deliberate, and emerges a one of the transcendent themes in both works. Ultimately, then, the inherent ambiguity of place as described by character reminds us that we are dealing with a work in an "unreliable mode" (Booth 39); hence evidence from such a source can never be decisive. At the same time, we are reminded that frequently there is a paradoxical interplay between reality and fiction in works of this mode, and that such an interplay is frequently at work in the fiction of Vargas Llosa.

In The Role of Place in Literature, Lutwack suggests that the twentieth century is a time of renewed interest in place as an important issue in general: "This is a result of widespread public recognition that earth as a place or the total environment, is being radically changed and perhaps rendered uninhabitable by more and more pervasive and powerful technologies" (2). The ensuing question of whether man can change his perception of himself in relation to his surroundings has resulted in an increased sensitivity to place, "sensitivity inspired by aesthetic as well as ecological values, imaginative as well as functional needs" (Lutwack 2). Such sensitivity is everywhere evident in Vargas Llosa's narrative. In Palomino Molero and Mayta, sensitivity to scene and the features of urban and rural landscapes convey aspects of character identity and the predominant themes. Simultaneously, plot provides a context and characters that help to clarify landscape. Such a dynamic process ultimately results in a unique image of a literary landscape while contributing to the development of a strong sense of place in the reader.

NOTES

[1] see René Wellek and Austin Warren, Theory of Literature, 3rd ed. (New York: Harcourt, 1957) 220-23.

[2] Leonard Lutwack, The Role of Place in Literature (Syracuse: Syracuse UP, 1984) 2.

[3] John S. Brushwood, The Spanish American Novel (Austin: U of Texas Press, 1975) 254. My emphasis.

[4] Dick Gerdes, Mario Vargas Llosa (Boston: G. K. Hall, 1985) 169.

[5] Raymond L. Williams, Mario Vargas Llosa (New York: Ungar, 1986) 50. My emphasis.

[6] Marvin A. Lewis, From Lima to Leticia: The Peruvian Novels of Mario Vargas Llosa (Lanham, MD: University Press of America, 1983).

[7] see Antonio Cornejo Polar, Revista de Crítica Literaria, no. 24 (1986): 283-4, and Julio Ortega, Revista Iberoamericana, no. 137 (octubre/diciembre 1986): 975-8.

[8] Roy C. Boland, "Demonios y lectores: génesis y reescritura de ¿Quíen mató a Palomino Molero?,"Antípodas, 1 (December 1988):180.

[9] José Miguel Oviedo, "Historia de Mayta: una reflexión política en forma de novela," Antípodas, 1 (December 1988):146.

[10] Wayne C. Booth, The Rhetoric of Fiction, 10th ed. (Chicago: U of Chicago Press, 1973) 175.

168

Index

Scripta Humanistica

Directed by
BRUNO M. DAMIANI
The Catholic University of America
COMPREHENSIVE LIST OF PUBLICATIONS *

BOOK ORDERS

* Clothbound. *All book orders*, except library orders, must be prepaid and addressed to **Scriptá Humanística**, 1383 Kersey Lane, Potomac, Maryland 20854. *Manuscripts* to be considered for publication should be sent to the same address.

www.ingramcontent.com/pod-product-compliance
Lightning Source LLC
Chambersburg PA
CBHW020355100426
42812CB00001B/62